Thinking About
Law and Ethics

Thinking About Law and Ethics

✦

Answers to Frequently Asked Questions with Case Examples

Ellsworth Lapham Fersch

iUniverse, Inc.
New York Lincoln Shanghai

Thinking About Law and Ethics
Answers to Frequently Asked Questions with Case Examples

iUniverse books may be ordered through booksellers or by contacting:

iUniverse
2021 Pine Lake Road, Suite 100
Lincoln, NE 68512
www.iuniverse.com
1-800-Authors (1-800-288-4677)

Because of the dynamic nature of the Internet, any Web addresses or links contained in this book may have changed since publication and may no longer be valid.

The information, ideas, and suggestions in this book are not intended to render legal advice. Before following any suggestions contained in this book, you should consult your personal attorney. Neither the author nor the publisher shall be liable or responsible for any loss or damage allegedly arising as a consequence of your use or application of any information or suggestions in this book.

ISBN: 978-0-595-47673-2 (pbk)
ISBN: 978-0-595-91939-0 (ebk)

Printed in the United States of America

Contents

Ethics and Law

Basic Issues

Administrative Issues

About the Book

This volume grew out of my Harvard course on Law and Ethics, subtitled Making the Moral Decision, and is modeled on three earlier books that answered approximately one hundred frequently asked questions and featured approximately fifteen case examples about the insanity defense, and the sexually dangerous, and psychopaths and psychopathy. This book follows a somewhat similar organization to those, though the case examples here are incorporated within the questions and answers, of which there are double the number in the previous books. Many of the case examples are court cases and they are surrounded by explanatory legal and ethical materials. Also, because the answer to each question is self-contained and because readers may choose to explore the book in various ways, some materials are repeated where necessary to answer each question. For simplicity, the masculine pronoun has been used throughout when both males and females may be involved. On some occasions, a plural accompanies a singular to make the same point.

Although this volume includes an extensive Bibliography, it does not refer specifically to every listing within the text itself. Intended for the general reader and student, and not for the researcher or the scholar, this volume assists that reader in thinking about legal and moral decision making by presenting varying approaches to the materials. At the same time, it provides a more comprehensive list of references for those who may wish to examine further some aspect of the topics. Everyone who reads this book is encouraged to explore at length the original sources from the U.S. Supreme Court and elsewhere for their interpretations, rationales, and particular styles. It is my hope that this volume will encourage all readers to pursue further the many topics in law and ethics about which we hear and see so much, and which impact so many lives, including our own.

Search engines today make continuing that exploration readily available to everyone. While many sources for the stories, cases, quotations, approaches, and assessments in this book are specifically referenced in the Bibliography and others are referred to throughout the text, the following were, and will be, especially helpful in the effort to locate greater detail or to update these materials: *The New York Times*; *The Wall Street Journal*; *The Chronicle of Higher Education*; *The Harvard Crimson*; *The Boston Globe*; CBS's *60 Minutes*; ABC's *Nightline*; and oyez.org, through which U.S. Supreme Court cases, oral arguments, and multi-media can be accessed.

Because the gathering of the materials included in this volume had to rely on reports from a variety of sources, and because those who participated directly in the various cases and examples presented as well as those who commented on and analyzed them had their own definite perspectives, a cautionary note is in order about the material in this book. The facts and the conclusions in all of the topics may interact in limited or biased ways. Facts may lead toward conclusions, or conclusions may require the refitting of facts. The arguments for each side of each of these controversial topics may use facts in a relatively straight-forward way or they may bend them to bolster conclusions drawn with or without them. The inclusion of any individual or organization is not meant to imply that their views are necessarily fully represented. Their inclusion, instead, is meant to signal that this volume attempts to explore as broadly as possible the important topic of moral and legal decision making.

Once again, Alexander Blenkinsopp assisted in the editing of this volume as he had with the three previous books in the *Thinking About* series. His studies at and degrees from Harvard University and the University of Oxford combined criminology, law, ethics, and social studies; and his prowess in international debate and in written work won him outstanding honors in European competitions as they had in American competitions.

About the Author

Ellsworth Lapham Fersch has taught at Harvard University in the Medical and Extension Schools and in the College in the three decades since receiving his J.D. in law and his Ph.D. in clinical psychology there. His prior studies in English were at Yale University where he received his bachelor's degree, and at the University of California, Berkeley, where he received his master's on a Woodrow Wilson Fellowship. He has been a visiting faculty member at various colleges and universities including Wheaton College, Boston University, Yale University, and the University of Massachusetts. A licensed clinical psychologist and member of the Massachusetts Bar, he served as a long-time director of the Massachusetts Court Clinic. He maintains a private practice, and his teaching and writing concern topics at the intersection of ethics, law, psychology, and social policy. As General Editor of the three previous volumes in this series, *Thinking About the Insanity Defense*, *Thinking About the Sexually Dangerous*, and *Thinking About Psychopaths and Psychopathy*, he guided their preparation in his seminars, contributed material, and wrote their introductions. This volume grew out of his many-year Harvard course on Law and Ethics: Making the Moral Decision.

Introduction

Almost everyone has an opinion about almost every topic contained in this book, and even after reading such a book or taking a course that incorporates these materials, most do not, in my experience, change their overall view of these topics. Though some may vary their view a bit, the weight of their history and family and environment and experience, even their brains and genes, has solidified their views. Their views may be consistent with one another or even contradictory, but on each topic they consider their conclusion to be the moral one. For almost everyone, then, the conclusions they reach about the most important life and death issues (as abortion, the care of children, capital punishment, and the right to die) and about the most significant administrative topics (as affirmative action, professional conduct, sexual conduct, and privacy) appear to them to be moral decisions. And they are, for them, and for a variety of reasons that we will explore in this book.

Further, general or more detailed acquaintance with these topics is widespread. For these topics headline the news, and occupy ordinary people as well as governmental, business, educational, and other leaders. Most of them cause serious controversies between and within religions and courts and legislatures and families as they impact the autonomy of the individual when it conflicts with the wishes of the majority. All of them concern everyone who must deal with basic life and death issues, as everyone must to a larger or lesser extent; and many concern those whose lives are impacted by important administrative issues as well. Because there is misinformation in society, in the media, even among lawyers and ethicists about all the topics, this book attempts to clarify the relevant moral and legal concerns.

Because the book is about moral decision making it is instructive to ask those who are making decisions whether others who directly oppose their view can also be making the moral decision. In response, some will say no, some will say yes, some are unsure. Why this is so and what it means is the broad subject of this book.

Let me begin with an imperfect analogy. Judges instruct juries before they begin their deliberations to discuss the case at some length prior to taking any sort of vote. Jurors are cautioned against beginning with a vote of the members.

The theory behind this suggested restriction is that individuals who take a position at the outset may be reluctant to back down from their stated view. They may be acting on limited information; they may have a skewed view of the case; they may be mistaken on some of the facts, theories, evidence, people in the matter. Even so, they may feel, as the deliberations proceed, that they need to justify their initial statement or view or vote. Yet the very process of coming to a unanimous verdict in a criminal case, for example, is to convince those who take a different position at the outset to move toward one consensus conclusion. And that is usually in the direction of the majority of jurors when the first vote was initially taken, whether at the beginning of deliberations or later on during them.

In the award-winning drama, *12 Angry Men*, a jury's initial vote of 11-1 for a guilty verdict and the ensuing resistance to and process of change were convincingly portrayed. While the outcome of the jury deliberation was contrary to the usual result in a vote skewed as that one initially was, the psychological processes at work remain valid and compelling.

That script began with a judge giving overall instructions to jurors at the end of a murder trial where the mandatory punishment for a guilty verdict was death. Jurors then retired to the jury room, elected a foreman, and took an immediate vote. In it, all jurors save one considered the defendant guilty. The entire drama then centered around that lone juror arguing his position, questioning the evidence, and gradually persuading the others, generally one by one, to change their vote from guilty to not guilty. He did this by essentially taking the role of a defense attorney questioning the evidence brought out at the trial but presumably left unaddressed in the courtroom itself. As the jurors sized up the arguments and each other, they shifted their votes until at the end of the drama, all voted the defendant not guilty. And audiences over the more than fifty years since its first production have felt that the final verdict was a just one. The drama was satisfying both because of the intricacies of the script and its questioning of eyewitness identification evidence and because those whose initial change encouraged others to change have been seen as more thoughtful, more balanced, less prejudiced, more humane, more moral it would appear. While psychologists often noted that that strong movement in this drama from 11-1 in one direction to all 12 in the opposite direction was highly unusual, they also noted that the social psychological processes at work in the group were the usual ones in any group. That psychological truth was what made the drama compelling and ultimately convincing for while the result may have been at odds with the likely movement within a group, the two common processes in any group were effectively portrayed.

Two psychological processes made the deliberations in *12 Angry Men* and the conclusion reached at its end understandable and compelling. While each juror came to the deliberation with his own views, approaches, history, experiences, knowledge, and sense of justice, the working out of those two processes made the drama especially effective and enduring. The first of these might be termed an expansion of views and the second might be called a comparison of those who hold the differing views.

The first social psychological process opened the members of the jury to a variety of different views, approaches, comments, even tentative conclusions, so that each one of them had a broader array of views to consider than he initially brought with him into the jury room. That is the variety that a book like this, or a course, or a discussion group, or a panel, or the immersion in a college or a different culture can accomplish. This book presents an extensive array of materials and it draws on many different sources. It accepts the challenge of going beyond what many may consider the true or moral or ethical or right answers to the questions which are raised in order to show the wide array of answers others consider to be true or moral or right ones. While some of the materials may immediately strike some readers as too far apart from their own views to be worthy even of consideration, the attempt here is to present as varying a range of views as have been addressed by legal and ethical commentators, by courts, by individuals and groups. The aim is to expand those materials which may prove to be of use in thinking about moral decision making, if not in making actual moral decisions.

The second psychological process on display in *12 Angry Men* was different from the presentation of an array of arguments, positions, evidence, approaches. It was more personal in that it allowed the members of the jury to experience for themselves which members held which views, which members argued more persuasively, which members had clearer understandings of the evidence, which members appeared more moral, and then having assessed the other members of the jury, to determine which persons' views they felt most comfortable with. That second process helped to explain why those who enter a new group often seek a group most like themselves or may, in entering a larger or smaller group unlike themselves, at least initially modify somewhat their own views, approaches, conclusions as they identify with some in the group more than with others.

Like the jury's deliberation, the initial purpose of this book is to expand the range of arguments, evidence, comment, approaches to topics at the intersection of law and ethics. When used in conjunction with a course its purpose is to guide that expansion so that those participating can determine which arguments seem more compelling, which persons they more easily identify with, and what influence the arguments and the persons have on the reader or the course-taker. Unlike jury deliberations, there is no need here to reach a consensus on moral decision making, and general moral views are less subject to change than are decisions about facts of a case in relation to the law governing them in a jury trial.

Originally, I compiled a draft version of some of these kinds of materials into a volume called *Making the Moral Decision* because that was the subtitle of the course I inherited whose main title was Law and Ethics. And yet, even at the outset, I wondered: What does it mean to make *the* moral decision? For that question implies strongly that there can be only one decision which is the moral one and that other offered decisions are necessarily therefore non-moral or immoral or amoral.

This book addresses that important question of what it means to make the moral decision by focusing on a number of current moral problems, and by examining various approaches to moral decision making. But the book reframes the question as it should be, if the purpose is educational and not indoctrinal. So, at the outset, the question should be: What does it mean to make *a* moral decision? For it is essentially the difference between *the* moral decision and *a* moral decision that captures the controversies now surrounding such issues as abortion and affirmative action and euthanasia and capital punishment and sexual conduct and the other topics included in this volume. What is the moral decision to make concerning abortion, for example? Or what is a moral decision to make concerning abortion, and can another decision which is directly opposed to that one also be a moral decision? Or can there be only one moral decision? This broad ranging inquiry is a large part of the controversy surrounding moral decision making.

This book aims to present, explain, question, and compare the various answers given to the contemporary moral questions raised. Among them are these. Should a woman have a right to an abortion? What are the limits on parents' choice of care for their children? Should there be capital punishment? Does a person have a right to die? Should there be affirmative action? What are the limits of professional conduct? What are permissible forms of sexual conduct? How much privacy should an individual be entitled to? Which ethical theories ought to prevail? Whose religious tradition ought to be controlling? How should the U.S. Constitution be interpreted? How should Judges decide?

To all of these questions there are opposing answers strongly advocated by those of varying views. Looming over all these problem areas is the still larger question of whether all of the opposing answers to these questions are moral answers, or whether each question can only be answered by one moral answer with the other answer either less moral or even immoral? And what is totally outside the realm of moral decision making? Certainly all decent, ethical, reasonable people would agree that genocide (as in the systematic killing of Jews, gypsies, homosexuals, and others in the Holocaust) is totally immoral.

But even where there appears to be but one moral decision, there can be disagreements about moral decision making. For while it is agreed that the genocide as demonstrated in the Holocaust is immoral, there are not many issues on which there is such unanimity in moral decision making. And even with the topic of genocide, there is disagreement. While ethicists agree that genocide is immoral, there are definitional disputes as to what is or what is not genocide. One such dispute arose within the Jewish Anti-Defamation League over whether to call the slaughter of Armenians by Ottoman Turks a genocide. And the House of Representatives and the President of the United States disagreed about whether to apply that term to that historical event, the former declaring it should be applied and the latter that it should not be.

People of good will who are decent, ethical, and reasonable people argue strongly the opposing sides of the major moral problems facing societies and individuals. Many follow the dictates of their own religion or their own sense of morality. When that does not conflict with the law, individuals can follow for themselves any acceptable set of moral values. Thus, many Roman Catholics and Evangelical Christians and others argue against a woman's right to an abortion while many Protestants, Jews, and others argue for a woman's right to abortion. All feel they are religious, moral people. Some minorities argue against affirmative action while their leaders and many of them argue for it. Both groups feel they are ethical people engaged in making the moral decision, yet they take opposing views. In the larger view, all are making a moral decision; yet in the view of those who hold one view (as, for example, those who completely oppose abortion) they are making the only possible moral decision. They feel that any view other than their view is an immoral one. And when the power of religion, for example, is not strong enough to compel people of their own faith or of other faiths to follow some particular moral view, then the effort is made, through the legislature or through the courts, to enact into law that group's view of the moral course of action. In a pluralistic society, one which guarantees the freedom of religion, the decision to enforce a particular moral view cannot be directly a religious one.

But that is not to say that religion does not play a strong role in determining what view the law will incorporate into its statutes, regulations, and court decisions. In the area of basic issues religion has always played a strong, if not dominant role while in the area of administrative issues, the influence of religion has been more subtle. And, of course, in a pluralistic society such as the United

States, secular humanism and various ethical constructs may be as important as or more important than religion.

Many times, people argue not about the moral decision but about which issues are within or outside the realm of moral discourse or, perhaps, near the edge of that realm. When the Pope declared at the United Nations that the protection of the environment was a moral cause for the Roman Catholic Church did that make it one to those outside the Church? Would a law mandating English as the national language, for example, be within or outside the realm of moral decision making? Whether or not something is within that realm, it may be an important issue to many people. So one might ask what difference it makes if an issue is viewed as a moral one or not. Perhaps it makes a difference in the seriousness with which the issue is taken. Perhaps it makes a difference in the kinds of arguments used to persuade. Perhaps it makes a difference in the urgency of the competing views. Not only do people argue about which issues dictate a clear decision based on a communal morality, but they take strongly divergent stances on just what is a communal morality, and who should decide what it is.

This book is designed to encourage moral reasoning, to set forth the arguments on various sides of issues, to encourage walking in others' shoes to understand more clearly the kinds of arguments being made and their implications for ethical and legal decision making. Clearly, the book is not a catechism. It attempts to avoid preaching a truth to be memorized and believed. For that exercise the reader must look elsewhere, and I have cited in the Bibliography a number of works of varying approaches to aid with that further exploration.

This book is intended for general reading on the topics covered, and for use in courses in Moral Problems, Ethical or Moral Reasoning, in Current Affairs, or in Law and Ethics. It does not presuppose prior work in either law or ethics. The focus is on cases and accompanying materials representing eight major moral problems: abortion, affirmative action, capital punishment, care of children, privacy, professional conduct, right to die, and sexual conduct. Half of these problems involve fundamental issues of life and death, while half involve important administrative practices in education, business, the professions, and at home. Some cases are drawn from contemporary events which have not found their way to court. These cases are summarized from media and other sources. Other cases have found their way to court. These cases are presented through majority and dissenting opinions of justices in courts in which the cases have been heard or to which they have been appealed.

In this book, cases have been summarized concisely to focus on the major arguments concerning the moral issues, the various lines of reasoning, and some of the examples and data used. Accompanying materials help to frame the issues, draw the arguments, and show varying approaches. The focus on the media and on courts reflects the most prominent sources for most people of guidance and debate on issues of law and ethics. This book emphasizes both the approaches to the problems and the content of the problems themselves. For in moral decision making there is controversy concerning the approaches taken as well as the conclusions drawn.

In concluding this introduction I should add that I have had direct personal experience with some of this material. Three of the case studies in this book involved me in lesser or greater ways. In one of them the son of the convicted and imprisoned judge who sought reinstatement to the bar was my teaching assistant and then the sponsor of seminars I gave at Yale during his time there, and I came to know him and his family well. In another of them my mother was scheduled to be operated on by the same doctor whose malpractice record was the subject of a *60 Minutes* broadcast I had used in my Law and Ethics course, and years later I was given his name as one of two possible consults for my own herniated disk. And in the third, I knew the judge conducting the inquest into the death of a young child of Christian Science parents, and had told him about my use of a case from the Massachusetts Cape in my Law and Ethics course. Beyond that kind of involvement, I have followed all the cases in the book and many others over some decades of interest and teaching. My own educational background in literature, clinical psychology, and law; my experience in courts and colleges; my personal religious and secular background; and even my initial courses, as a freshman in college, in ethics and in logic, have all contributed to my own views. The aim of this book, however, is not to display those views so much as it is to address the wide range of approaches, conclusions, and comments about these essential topics for individuals and for society. Toward that end, I attempt to present a balanced view, realizing that in our adversary system of justice, one view is inevitably pitted against its opposing view, and that the pendulum, as they say, swings from one conclusion to another over longer or shorter periods of time. That is part of what makes these topics invigorating and their study a challenge. I hope that reading this book will contribute to greater understanding of moral and legal issues, and to a wider appreciation of moral and ethical reasoning and of the role of law with individuals and with society.

Ethics and Law

1

Ethics

How can ethical problems be addressed and what sources advocate their solutions?

Before even considering the role of law in these contemporary problems, it is essential to consider ethical approaches by themselves, for there are many ways to address the problems and many sources advocating their solution.

What does the word moral mean?

According to the *American Heritage Dictionary of the English Language*, moral, as an adjective, means among other things, "Of or concerned with the judgment of the goodness or badness of human action and character" and "Conforming to standards of what is right or just in behavior." "Moral applies to personal character and behavior, especially sexual conduct." Synonyms include "ethical, virtuous, righteous."

How are ethics and morals related?

Though the terms ethics and morals have differing meanings they are, of course, related. Ethics is the study of what is right and what is good, and the study of ethics does focus on morals and moral issues. A difference, however, is that professions, such as law and medicine, have codes of ethics, violations of which make the professionals unethical. They do not have moral codes or codes of morality. Those are more general, but they are not what those wishing to be admitted to the bar or to the practice of medicine are tested on. Rather candidates are tested on their specific ethical codes, elements of which appear contrary to general morality or perhaps common sense. But those codes serve the purpose of the profession and must be learned and followed by the practitioners. Morals refers to the standards which individuals are told to or do observe in their conduct. Moral refers to the individual's capacity to make judgments concerning what is right and what is good. Moral also refers to the person whose behavior is consistent with ethical standards. The moral person makes right decisions and behaves in a way that is right and good.

What are the major sources of ethics?

Those broad ranging words, right and good, have proven to be anything but clear and straightforward. The content of those words have engaged philosophers, religious figures, businessmen, educators, writers and citizens in a great and continual debate. Standard texts of ethics have tended to focus on Western thinkers and have included the definitions and explanation of the right and the good as set forth by such diverse figures as Aristotle, Jesus Christ, Thomas Hobbes, Immanuel Kant, John Stuart Mill, Plato, Jean Paul Sartre, and St. Augustine. Ethical theories have included such varying accounts as Christianity, Judaism, Hedonism, Libertarianism, Self Realization, and Utilitarianism, to name but a few.

In discussing moral problems, however, most writers on applied ethics do not discuss specific moral philosophies or specific religious or psychological beliefs. Rather, they tend to write in more general terms, to use the words moral or immoral as if the reader understood and agreed with whatever meaning the writer had. When specific moral views are mentioned they tend to be references to utilitarianism or retributivism; when specific religious views are mentioned they tend to be Roman Catholic or Basic Christian views.

In attempting to understand or advocate the moral decision, individuals and groups take many moral outlooks. In this book, a number of those will be identified and briefly described. Those views can then be used to reflect upon the case materials which follow.

To what extent has religion been a major source of morality and the basis for ethical codes of conduct?

Religion has always formed the basis for many peoples conclusions about morality and ethics. The major religions, Judaism, Christianity, Islam, Hinduism, Buddhism, Confucianism, all have their adherents throughout the world and all make clear their view of the moral life.

What were the religious affiliations of adults in the world?

The estimated percentage in 2004 of adults adhering to religions affiliations in the world were Christianity, 33; Islam, 20; Hinduism, 13; Buddhism, 6; Sikhism 0.4; Judaism, 0.2.

Since the founding of the United States, what has been its predominant religious tradition?

In the United States, the major religious views have been, since the founding, those of the Judeo-Christian tradition, especially of the Christian component. Viewed as one tradition, these ethics regard love as the highest good, as the measure of moral worth, and individuals as of infinite value; they rest moral constructs on the blessed person of the Beatitudes, the imperatives of the Ten Commandments, and the simple statement of the Golden Rule of doing unto others as one would have the others do unto oneself.

More specifically, within the Christian tradition, there are many variations. Three widely followed variations are Roman Catholic ethics, which include opposition to abortion, homosexuality, and same-sex marriage, and adherence to the doctrine of the infallibility of the Pope, among other values; fundamentalist and more conservative Protestant Christian ethics, which have become well known through their stands on religious, political, and social issues, including opposition to abortion, homosexuality, and various equal rights provisions; and more liberal Protestant ethics which support abortion, and often homosexuality.

Joining the Pope who declared that abortion was "not a human right" and the Roman Catholic Church in their teaching that homosexuality was sinful was the head of the Russian Orthodox Church who declared homosexuality to be both a sin and an illness. He reportedly said while speaking in Europe that homosexuality was a "distortion of the human personality, like kleptomania."

Within the Jewish tradition there are also more conservative and more liberal views. The moral views of Orthodox Judaism are roughly comparable to Roman Catholics; of Conservative Judaism, Episcopalianism; of Reform Judaism, less rigid Protestant denominations as far as Unitarianism; of Chassidim, to some cults.

There are no Judaic or Christian forms comparable to secular humanism.

What are the religious affiliations of the U.S. Supreme Court Justices?

All Supreme Court Justices profess faith and adhere to the Judeo-Christian tradition. Five are Roman Catholic. They are Chief Justice John Roberts, and Associate Justices Antonin Scalia, Clarence Thomas, Anthony Kennedy, and Samuel Alito. Two Associate Justices are Protestant, David Souter who is Episcopalian, and John Paul Stevens who is Baptist. And two Associate Justices, Stephen Breyer and Ruth Bader Ginsburg, are Jewish.

Among the questions raised by religion are these. To what extent ought religion and moral good to be similar? Who is to decide what part of religion ought to be retained as moral imperative and what part rejected? How separable are the moral mandates of religion in general and of specific religions?

What is the relation between one's own personal religion, and one's role as a Supreme Court Justice, or as a legislator?

When John F. Kennedy ran for President of the United States he said that he would not let his Roman Catholic faith interfere with the oath of office he took to defend the Constitution of the United States. When John F. Kerry ran for President of the United States he said that, even though a Roman Catholic, he supported a woman's right to choose whether or not to have an abortion but that he believed that life began at conception. Obviously, the two views logically conflicted with each other, and the second fit the Roman Catholic Church view while the first clearly did not. As a consequence of his support for abortion rights, some Roman Catholics said he should be denied communion because that support for abortion rights, and for homosexual rights as well, contradicted the Church's moral position. Kerry was labeled, as many are, a cafeteria Catholic, choosing the parts of doctrine that he supported and rejecting the others.

With five Roman Catholics among the nine justices on the U.S. Supreme Court, one might ask of them the question that was initially asked of John F. Kennedy. What is the relation between their own faith and their role as Supreme Court Justice? In essence, they may be either what are termed cafeteria Catholics if they vote more liberally on such matters as abortion and homosexuality or they are adherents of the moral prescriptions of their faith if they vote more conservatively on those matters.

And with one Episcopalian on the Court, the question occurs: To what extent will a split in the Anglican Communion affect his moral decision making? The split involved a group of Anglican archbishops who objected to the ordination by the Episcopal Church in America of a homosexual and who were affiliating with the Anglican churches in Kenya and elsewhere in Africa to avoid what they considered the moral permissiveness in America. They wanted either to transform or to replace the Episcopal Church. It was said that they wanted to gain the moral and symbolic power of asserting that they agreed with the majority of Anglicans in the world, and also that other Protestant denominations, especially Methodists, Lutherans, and Presbyterians, would be following the results of their actions.

The role of religion is less than clear, however. Since the reasons given for their votes do not generally cite their religious views as the basis of their moral decision making, one can only make assumptions about the place of faith in their legal decisions. On occasion, however, as in Justice Burger's concurring opinion in Bowers v. Hardwick, the religious rationale was more clearly detailed. On the whole, though, it remained implicit rather than explicit.

What were the religious affiliations of adults in the United States?

Based on their self-identification, the estimated percentage in 2004 of adults adhering to religions affiliations in the United States were: Christianity, 76.5; Non-religious/Secular, 13.2; Judaism, 1.3; Islam, 0.5; Agnostic, 0.5; Atheist, 0.4; Hinduism, 0.3; Unitarian Universalist, 0.3; Wiccan/Pagan/Druid, 0.1; Spiritualist, 0.05; Native American Religion, 0.05; Bahai, 0.04.

What is Puritanism?

Puritanism, which denoted a strictness or austerity in conduct and religion, and which was termed by its supporters a morally rigorous approach to life's issues, and by its detractors a rigid moralism, remained an influential force in American religion and ethics; and its hostility to social pleasures was an important element of religious and governmental practices throughout the world. The American writer H.L. Mencken once mocked Puritanism as "the haunting fear that someone, somewhere may be happy."

What major philosophical views inform moral decision making on these issues?

The major Western philosophical views relevant to these materials included the following. The ethics of utilitarianism featured Jeremy Bentham's and John Stuart Mill's advocacy of the greatest good for the greatest number, and the view that actions which tended to produce happiness were right, while those that promoted pain were wrong. The ethics of the categorical imperative focused on Immanuel Kant's maxim to act only if one can will that such an act become a universal law, and concluded that what was moral was what could be universally applied to all. The ethics of justice focused on Rawls' contribution which stated that justice was fairness, and that what was moral was what was fair. And some would add the ethics of retributivism, which concluded that it was moral to receive one's just desserts.

What did a psychologist term the five moral systems?

Based on his research, as reported in *The Happiness Hypothesis*, a psychologist detected five moral systems. The two most important were embodied in the precepts "do no harm" and "do unto others as you would they unto you" (termed the Golden Rule); the three others were "protect the group," show "loyalty," and have "respect for authority and purity." Some responded by saying that the first two were moral values, while the remaining three were ideological values.

What were termed the six methods of moral reasoning?

In his book, *A Question of Values*, Hunter Lewis outlined what he called modes or techniques of moral reasoning. He explained six categories. They included authority, deductive logic, sense experience, emotion, intuition, and science. He said each was used as a guide to ethics and morality.

Lewis argued that these six modes of moral reasoning underlay the value systems which we follow. He said that the values themselves were inextricably tied to the modes of reasoning. In his book, he explained the values a chapter at a time. A brief view of each follows.

What is authority?

Those who rely on authority to help them make the moral decision may turn to some external source such as religion or a university. They may turn to a religious text such as the *Holy Bible* or the *Talmud* or the *Koran* or the *Book of Mormon* or *Science and Health with Key to the Scriptures*, or to a secular text such as Mill's *On Liberty*, or as discussed in some length, to such legal texts as U.S. Supreme Court decisions. They may turn to a religious figure such as the Pope, the Dalai Lama, the Ayatollah, or to L. Ron Hubbard or Mary Baker Eddy. They may turn to a political figure such as a President or a statesperson. They may turn to a general or political philosophy such as utilitarianism or socialism. They may even turn to someone who has presented himself as an authority though only his followers may think that. The authorities that people turn to for guidance in making the moral decision are vast, though many people turn to but a few of those listed.

What is logic?

Those who rely on logic tend to look for consistency in moral positions. They rely on a structured thought process in their examination.

What is sense experience?

Those who rely on sense experience rely primarily on their own five senses to determine what is moral and what the moral decision should be. They may expand beyond their own senses to include what the culture itself concludes.

What is emotion?

Those who rely on emotion use their feelings to help them determine what seems right. They tend to employ empathy and to feel more strongly about matters concerning their own sub-group.

What is intuition?

Those who rely on intuition to make the moral decision let their unconscious mind work to cause them to arrive at their conclusion in what appears to be an instant. Some applied philosophers say that they begin with their intuition and then reason logically from there.

What is science?

Those who rely on science test hypotheses by collecting data and examining them. Lewis included both social and physical science within this category and stated that it combined other methods of moral reasoning: sense experience to gather facts and later to test the results; intuition to determine what to test; and logic to design the test.

How are these methods of moral reasoning combined?

In some instances modes are combined. Beyond the combinatory category of science, Lewis examined what he termed composite value systems. Among these were classical liberalism, now often termed libertarianism with its emphasis on liberty; classical conservatism with its emphasis on the group; legalism which he termed the religion of the law. He said there are many others and detailed a number of them.

What about Harvard's requirement in moral/ethical reasoning?

Lewis also examined Harvard's requirement in moral/ethical reasoning. He said that because of Harvard's diversity and pluralism, the moral reasoning requirement has had to concentrate on deductive logic rather than on moral precepts as might be gained from deference to authority or through some of the other methods of making the moral decision.

What about applied ethics?

Finally, as regards applied ethics, of which this book is an example, Lewis said that "Teaching students about verbal clarity, consistency, the avoidance of logical fallacies, the application of these skills to real life all this is potentially invaluable." He called it a modest exercise but one with realistic chances of successful completion.

What are some related approaches to and topics in moral decision making?

In addition to these approaches to moral reasoning, there are a number of specific questions often addressed in focusing on current moral problems. They include the use of analogies and extremes, as well as the topics of privacy, personhood, paternalism, religion, and the law itself.

What about the use of analogies and extremes?

The use of analogies and extremes raises a number of questions. What analogies can be made to comparable moral or social situations to help understand the moral problem under consideration? What parallels clarify the discussion of moral issues? What are the limits to the use of analogies? And what happens when moral arguments are carried to their logical extremes? Is that a helpful tool toward making the moral decision?

What about privacy?

Similarly, privacy raises questions. What is the nature of privacy? What ought to be the limits of privacy? How ought individuals to be able to control their own privacy? How is privacy to be balanced with security?

What about personhood?

Among the questions raised by personhood are these. What does it mean to be a person? What rights ought persons to have? What would deprive an individual of personhood? What would determine the beginning of personhood?

What about paternalism?

Questions include these. To what extent ought the state to protect people from themselves? To what extent ought adults to be treated as autonomous beings capable of making their own decisions for themselves? In balancing freedom and risk to what extent is it important to ask what kind of harm, how much harm, how likely the harm, what is the fallout from the harm, what good comes with the harm, how knowledgeable is the individual concerning the harm?

What about codes of ethics for the professions?

Medicine and psychology and law all have codes of ethics to govern their professionals. As I noted in *Who is the Client?* psychologists (and by extension psychiatrists) have difficult ethical issues to address as they serve the legal system while acting as psychoforensic professionals within it and as clinical professionals within their own discipline. As the American Psychological Association's Ethics Director noted in his Ethics Rounds column in the *Monitor on Psychology*, "A theme that has become central to our work in providing consultation is identifying and distinguishing the ethical, legal, and clinical aspects of the question posed." He continued by saying, "clarifying what questions need to be asked can also offer a structured path for resolving the dilemma with which the psychologist is struggling." One of the two kinds of calls that the Association Ethics Office often received involved a matter dealt with in this book, the question of mandatory child-abuse reporting. The Director stated that "the ethical follows upon the legal which, in turn, follows upon the clinical." And he concluded: "An overarching message is that legal and ethical dilemmas never arise in a vacuum. They arise in the course of our work as psychologists. Our background, training, and experience as psychologists are therefore always central in formulating our ethical response."

What did the American Medical Association consider the principles of medical ethics?

The American Medical Association's statement began: "The medical profession has long subscribed to a body of ethical statements developed primarily for the benefit of the patient. As a member of this profession, a physician must recognize responsibility to patients first and foremost, as well as to society, to other health professionals, and to self. The following Principles adopted by the American Medical Association are not laws, but standards of conduct which define the essentials of honorable behavior for the physician."

They included, among other characteristics, competence, compassion, professionalism, respect for law, confidentiality, and service to the individual and to society.

A brief example of ethical and legal issues in medical misconduct concerned the former president of the Harvard affiliated teaching hospital McLean. After Dr. Jack Gorman admitted to New York regulators that he had had inappropriate sexual contact with a patient, his medical license was suspended in New York.

The Massachusetts Department of Public Health then directed McLean Hospital to investigate whether Gorman's misleading them at the time of his appointment and his conduct during his brief tenure there, had further violated professional ethical and legal standards.

What six principles were often considered the core of medical ethics?

The six fundamental principles of medical ethics were described by many, using these words: beneficence, non-maleficence, autonomy, justice, dignity, and truth or honesty. The first two referred to doing good and doing no harm; the third to preserving a sense of self; the fourth and fifth to fairness and respect for the individual; and the last to integrity.

What did the Rules of Professional Conduct declare to be the standards for lawyers?

The Preamble to the Massachusetts Rules of Professional Conduct set forth lawyers' responsibilities. These included competently, diligently, and promptly representing clients; keeping their confidences; respecting and adhering to the law; being "guided by personal conscience and the approbation of professional peers."

The Rules acknowledged that "Virtually all difficult ethical problems arise from conflict between a lawyer's responsibilities to clients, to the legal system, and to the lawyer's own interest in remaining an upright person while earning a satisfactory living."

The Preamble assured that "The Rules of Professional Conduct prescribe terms for resolving such conflicts. Within the framework of these Rules, many difficult issues of professional discretion can arise. Such issues must be resolved through the exercise of sensitive professional and moral judgment guided by the basic principles underlying the Rules."

What did the Code of Judicial Conduct declare to be the standards for judges?

The Massachusetts Code of Judicial Conduct, similar to other states' codes, listed in its first three canons the guiding principles for judges. Those Canons declared that a judge should "uphold the integrity and independence of the judiciary," "avoid impropriety and the appearance of impropriety," and "perform the duties of his office impartially and diligently." The remaining canons addressed fiscal responsibilities, non-political mandates, and administrative duties.

As a brief example of ethical and legal issues in judicial conduct, a federal judge rebuked Massachusetts state district court judge Diane Moriarty, without naming her, for vacating a previous state conviction against a drug dealer about to be sentenced in federal court. At the time she acted, without prosecutors present, the judge instructed the defendant's lawyer to inform his client that "it was an early Christmas present." In the face of criticism that she had deviated from Massachusetts laws as well as from the Code of Judicial Conduct, the judge reversed herself, then took a leave of absence, for unspecified reasons, from the judiciary. Her initial action raised both ethical and legal issues.

2

Law

What is the relation of law to moral decision making?

In examining the relation between law and moral decision making, a number of essential questions are raised. What ought to be the relation between what is moral and what is legal? To what extent are they the same and to what extent different? How much smaller, or larger, ought the sphere of illegality to be than the sphere of immorality?

What law are we referring to?

This book will refer specifically to the law of the United States. Though material will address other law as well, it will largely focus on the U.S. Constitution.

The Founders of the United States drafted a Constitution and made provisions for Amendments to that Constitution. The Constitution and the Amendments form one source of law. State legislatures and the Federal legislature, the Congress, pass laws. They constitute another source of law. Agencies make regulations. They constitute another source of law. State courts interpret their own State Constitution and various laws, and Federal Courts interpret the Federal Constitution and various laws. All these constitute still another source of law.

What are the various levels of courts that may be involved in moral decision making?

A brief review of the state and federal systems shows that both generally have three levels of courts. At the lowest level are the trial courts that hear cases and render decisions about both criminal and civil matters, sometimes with a jury, sometimes by a judge, and usually focusing upon factual questions. Next higher are the intermediate appellate courts to which questions of law may be referred. Finally there is the highest appellate court, often called Supreme. In the United States, for example, it is the U.S. Supreme Court; in Massachusetts, it is called the Supreme Judicial Court. Occasionally the names of the courts are misleading but whatever they happen to be called they serve the same three functions. Justices of the U.S. Supreme Court are appointed for life. Judges in other courts may be limited by age, elected, appointed, or subject to election after appointment.

The highest level of the appellate courts are where the kinds of moral problems this book addresses are finally decided, and that is why they are featured here. Sometimes that highest court refuses to hear an appeal and as a consequence the decision of the intermediate appellate court remains as the answer to the legal and moral question(s) raised.

What about legislatures?

Courts are interpreting laws passed by democratically elected legislatures. The United States Congress has two separate bodies, the Senate, where each state has two Senators, and the House of Representatives, where each state has a number proportional to its population. Most states have two branches to their legislature, but that is not required. In the Federal system, the Senate must advise and consent on the appointment of U.S. Supreme Court justices and many other Executive branch appointments.

Do most cases which reach the U.S. Supreme Court or other federal or state appellate courts involve moral issues and the interpretation of the relevant Constitution?

The short answer is no. Most of the cases which the United States Supreme Court and other federal and state appellate courts decide do not involve the kinds of moral issues this book addresses. Because the language of statutes and regulations can be subjected to varying interpretations and because the body that drew them up may not have made clear its intention, courts become involved in resolving those disputes. Those disputes, however, are not what this book concerns.

This book, on the contrary, deals with great moral and ethical issues for which appellate courts seek guidance in the relevant constitutional document, and then explain their reasons for their legal decision making which includes the underlying explicit or implicit moral decision making.

For questions of moral decision making, what are the relevant Amendments to the United States Constitution?

For issues involving moral decision making, the most often relevant parts of the United States Constitution are the first ten Amendments to it, and the Fourteenth Amendment. The first ten Amendments to the United States Constitution are called the Bill of Rights. They became effective December 15, 1791. The Fourteenth Amendment was adopted in 1868. Each of them can be relevant to the kinds of topics covered in this book. A brief summary of each follows.

What is the First Amendment?

Congress shall make no law respecting an establishment of religion, or prohibiting the free exercise thereof; or abridging the freedom of speech or of the press; or the right of the people peaceably to assemble, and to petition the government for a redress of grievances.

What is the Second Amendment?

A well regulated militia being necessary to the security of a free state, the right of the people to keep and bear firearms shall not be infringed.

What is the Third Amendment?

No soldier shall, in time of peace, be quartered in any house without the consent of the owner, nor in time of war but in a manner prescribed by law.

What is the Fourth Amendment?

The right of the people to be secure in their persons, houses, papers, and effects, against unreasonable searches and seizures, shall not be violated, and no warrants shall issue but upon probable cause, supported by oath or affirmation, and particularly describing the place to be searched, and the persons or other things to be seized.

What is the Fifth Amendment?

No person shall be held to answer for a capital or other infamous crime unless on a presentment or indictment of a grand jury, except in cases arising in the land or naval forces, or in the militia, when in actual service, in time of war or public danger; nor shall any person be subject for the same offence to be twice put in jeopardy of life or limb; nor shall be compelled in any criminal case to be a witness against himself, nor be deprived of life, liberty, or property, without due process of law; nor shall private property be taken for public use without just compensation.

What is the Sixth Amendment?

In all criminal prosecutions, the accused shall enjoy the right to a speedy and public trial, by an impartial jury of the state and district wherein the crime shall have been committed, which district shall have been previously ascertained by law, and to be informed of the nature and cause of the accusation; to be confronted with the witnesses against him; to have compulsory process for obtaining witnesses in his favor, and to have the assistance of counsel for his defense.

What is the Seventh Amendment?

In suits at common law, where the value in controversy shall exceed twenty dollars, the right of trial by jury shall be preserved, and no fact tried by a jury shall be otherwise reexamined in any court of the United States than according to the rules of the common law.

What is the Eighth Amendment?

Excessive bail shall not be required, nor excessive fines imposed, nor cruel and unusual punishment inflicted.

What is the Ninth Amendment?

The enumeration in the Constitution of certain rights shall not be construed to deny or disparage others retained by people.

What is the Tenth Amendment?

The powers not delegated to the United States by the Constitution, nor prohibited by it to the states, are reserved to the states respectively, or to the people.

What is the Fourteenth Amendment?

Section 1. All persons born or naturalized in the United States, and subject to the jurisdiction thereof, are citizens of the United States and of the state wherein they reside. No state shall make or enforce any law which shall abridge the privileges or immunities of citizens of the United States; nor shall any state deprive any person of life, liberty, or property without due process of law; nor deny to any person within its jurisdiction the equal protection of the law.

What is Title VI of the Civil Rights Act of 1964?

Title VI of the Civil Rights Act of 1964 "prohibits discrimination on the basis of race, color, and national origin in programs and activities receiving federal assistance." While it prohibits intentional discrimination, funding agencies have regulations that prohibit practices that have the effect of discrimination.

What is Islamic Shariah law?

By those who follow it, Islamic Shariah law is considered comparable to Anglo-American common law and European civil law. Its goal in the criminal justice system is to protect religion, life, intellect, offspring, and property through punishment aimed at deterring others as well as punishing offenders.

The majority of Muslims surveyed in Arab countries and in other Muslim societies said they preferred that Islamic law be either a source, or the sole source, of legislation. By contrast, according to a report by the International Crisis Group, support for Islamic law in Turkey had never exceeded 20 percent. The vast historical differences between Turkey and the region's other countries had to be taken into account. A political party in Turkey had evolved to become more in line with Turkey's secular tradition. By contrast, it was said, secularism in the Arab world peaked in the 1950s and '60s, then stopped with the Six Day War of 1967. Some claimed that the Arabs' defeat then by Israel contributed to rise of political Islam. That has prospered since then.

Under Shariah law, if Islamists came to power in many Arab states they would likely ban alcohol, homosexuality, and what they considered pornographic images on the Internet and in film. And their definition is much more restrictive than the one provided by the U.S. Supreme Court.

What is the primary difference between the law of the United States and Islamic Shariah law?

The primary difference between the law of the United States and Islamic Shariah law is that in the United States religion and law are separate, as the First Amendment to the U.S. Constitution states: "Congress shall make no law respecting an establishment of religion, or prohibiting the free exercise thereof." In Islamic law, on the other hand, there is no separation of church and state. In fact, the religion of Islam and the government are one. The Islamic religion governs all governmental authority. Islamic law is therefore the direct opposite of United States law. That is not to say that United States law is not influenced by religion and by religious values, because, as many of the materials in this book attest, it is. But that influence must be by indirection, implicitly involved, whether acknowledged or not. Though the United States was founded by men within the Judeo-Christian tradition, and that tradition underlies much of the founding and history of the United States, there can be no official religion in the United States, government cannot favor one religion over another, and religious pluralism is tolerated, even encouraged. As a consequence, within the framework of the American democracy, Islamic law cannot be accepted. In majority-Islamic countries, which nonetheless practice democracy, religious pluralism can be found; in majority-Islamic countries, which do not practice democracy, religions besides Islam cannot be tolerated.

What is stare decisis in the law?

The Latin term stare decisis, which means to stand by things decided, is the principle that judicial precedents should be followed. Courts ought not lightly to overturn or reverse settled law. It is based on the idea that retaining settled law and interpretations allows everyone to plan more effectively to follow the law and thus encourages both law-abiding behavior and respect for the law.

What is stare indecisis?

The alteration of precedent by the Supreme Court in overruling a precedent has been termed stare indecisis in a book of that title.

How were Betts v. Brady and Gideon v. Wainwright examples of moral decision making?

To help understand what it means to make the moral decision, we start with the U.S. Supreme Court case of Gideon v. Wainwright, which incorporates elements from both law and ethics. Analyzing the case requires consideration of these questions. What is the decision the court makes in the case? What prior decision does it affirm or overrule? What explanation is given for the decision? To what extent do the justices agree among themselves concerning the decision? What are the elements of morality, or ethics, which are explicitly discussed in the opinions? What elements are implicitly contained in the opinions? How does legal reasoning differ from or concur with other forms of moral reasoning? And finally, who agrees with the decision, the reasoning, the implications, and the importance of the case for society? What is the aftermath of the case?

What did the case of Betts v. Brady decide about the right to counsel?

The 1942 case of Betts v. Brady concerned a man convicted of robbery. Unable to provide for a lawyer of his own, he sought appointment of one. The judge refused explaining that only prosecutions for murder and rape were given counsel. Betts defended himself and was found guilty. When his case reached the Supreme Court the majority held that, while the 14th Amendment to the U.S. Constitution required appointment of counsel for indigent defendants in federal criminal cases, refusal to appoint counsel for an indigent defendant charged with a felony did not necessarily violate the Due Process Clause of the Fourteenth Amendment. In explaining its decision, the majority referred to the Constitutions of the thirteen original states and found great diversity among them in their approach to the appointment of counsel in such cases. The Court also declared that it was a matter of legislative policy, and therefore not for the Court to decide, as to whether such defendants would have counsel appointed for them. The Court did not find the denial of counsel in such a case a matter of "fundamental fairness." They found the diverse decisions of the various legislatures Constitutionally sound. The dissenting justices, however, declared that the right to counsel in a criminal proceeding is a fundamental right. From 1942 until 1963, that decision in Betts v. Brady, drawn in general terms of federalism and diversity, and of fairness and right, remained the law. But that view of what is fair and what is right and whether there should be uniformity, changed in 1963 in the case of Gideon v. Wainwright. The Betts and Gideon cases, and commentaries on them, provide an important view of the influence of stability in the law, of the reasons for change, of the arguments for and against the concept of stare decisis.

What did the case of Gideon v. Wainwright decide about the right to counsel?

Almost twenty years later, the 1963 case of Gideon v. Wainwright closely paralleled the facts of the 1942 case of Betts v. Brady. Gideon was charged with robbery, requested and was denied appointment of counsel, conducted his own defense, was found guilty, and appealed the refusal to appoint counsel. Because the case raised the same question as Betts, and because Gideon now had appointed counsel, the question before the Supreme Court became "Should this Court's holding in Betts v. Brady (1942) be reconsidered?" In short, did an indigent defendant in a criminal trial have the right to an appointed counsel?

Had the Supreme Court followed the decision in Betts, the answer would have been no. But the Supreme Court overruled Betts. It stated unanimously that the answer was yes. The Court declared that what Gideon sought was a fundamental right essential to a fair trial, and that in state courts, as well as in federal courts, indigent defendants have that right. The Court did not employ stare decisis.

How did the Supreme Court explain its overruling of Betts v. Brady?

The Supreme Court said that it was returning to pre-Betts "old precedents, sounder we believe than the new." It further declared: "Not only these precedents but also reason and reflection require us to recognize that in our adversary system of criminal justice, any person haled into court, who is too poor to hire a lawyer, cannot be assured a fair trial unless counsel is provided him. This seems to us to be an obvious truth." Further, the decision said that earlier distinctions in Betts v. Brady had no basis in logic or in authority. To decide what was legally and morally required, then, the Supreme Court relied on precedents prior to Betts, on what they termed reason and reflection and logic and authority, as well as on what they considered the "obvious truth" of their conclusion. Since they ruled unanimously, they could say, at least among themselves, that their conclusion embodied an obvious truth. Beyond providing an emphasis to what they had ruled, those words add nothing to the process of deciding what is the moral response.

To what extent was the Court explicit in its statement of ethics or morality in the Gideon case?

It is important to note for our purposes that the word moral was not used in Gideon v. Wainwright, nor was the decision called ethical by the Supreme Court. Instead, the opinion referred to a "fair system of justice" and indicated that "reason and reflection" supported the decision. Though moral was not used, it was obvious that the various Justices were writing about a system of moral decision making whose hallmark was fairness. And in looking to logic and authority they referred specifically to two of the six modes of moral reasoning outlined by Hunter Lewis in his book, *A Question of Values*. The decision rendered in Betts v. Brady was unfair, the Justices said; that rendered in Gideon v. Wainwright was fair.

How did the book Gideon's Trumpet *explain the moral decision making in the Gideon case?*

While the case itself did not use the word moral, Anthony Lewis in his book on the case, *Gideon's Trumpet*, used that word in twelve different instances. Examining his use of the word moral helps us to understand the various meanings attributed to the word as courts, citizens, lawyers, and others attempt to make the moral decision. Lewis' use of the word moral seemed to have a number of different meanings. It could mean important and forceful and convincing as in his saying that the Chief Justice's influence in the Supreme Court depends on his "moral and intellectual power to persuade." It could mean honesty as in Gideon's appointed counsel's "moral problem," whether to seek out details about the case which would enable him to make a more narrow argument freeing Gideon rather than a larger argument which would overrule the precedent of Betts v. Brady. As it turned out in the case, the lawyer made the moral choice, sought the details, and found that Gideon would not have fit a specific exception, so the lawyer could make the larger argument for overruling Betts.

Further, it could mean religious or fundamentally religious as in Gideon's statement that his family's moral standards were those of the Calvary Baptist Church; or that there are higher morals in the Bible Belt.

Or it could refer to the public support for an issue after Courts "generate a broad moral concern" about an issue concerning which legislatures had not received any demand from their constituents. It could refer to what is right and what is good according to one's own philosophical or religious or other values, as in the statement that the ordinary citizen "did not feel the ethical imperative" of the racial question until the Court decided the school desegregation case in 1954, at which time the public saw "the moral issue in racial segregation, and began to give the Court's decision the support it needed."

Finally, according to Lewis, it could refer directly to making the moral decision as in his description of the best Supreme Court Justices as ones who had "the ability to perceive great moral truths and to articulate them in a way that excites the imagination of the citizen." Judging whether one makes the moral decision depended upon the evaluator's views of what is good and what is right, Anthony Lewis' view, in short, was that the U.S. Supreme Court should lead public opinion, not follow it; should educate through its own enlightened views; and should therefore be "a great teacher."

Why was there no dissent in the Gideon case?

According to Anthony Lewis, there was no dissent in the Gideon case because there had already been a good deal of opposition to the original decision handed down in Betts v. Brady; and lawyers, commentators, and the Court had been searching for a case which would allow that earlier case to be overruled. Simply put, many felt that Betts v. Brady had come to the wrong conclusion. The Court had not made a moral decision. Those who applauded the Court's decision in the Gideon case were pleased that the precedent should not stand in the way of a fair decision.

What did the Gideon case suggest concerning stare decisis?

As a result of that approbation, the Gideon case made an important statement about stare decisis, the legal principle that laws should not be lightly overturned. For stability in the law, and in knowing what the law is, and in planning according to the law, what has been decided should remain the law except in extreme cases. Yet, in the Gideon case, the earlier precedent was overruled.

Stare decisis, in other words, was considered by the Supreme Court and by Anthony Lewis less important than coming to a fair, just, and moral decision. Whether overruling is wise depends on the direction one prefers the law to take. So when the decision which might be overruled is preferred, then many point to the importance of stare decisis, to letting precedent stand. When the decision which might be overruled is not preferred, then many point to the need for a just and moral decision, and advocate overruling a precedent. As Senate confirmation hearings on those nominated for seats on the Supreme Court showed, this argument was especially strong where abortion was concerned. Those who, for example, agreed with the decision in Roe v. Wade, the case legalizing abortion, argued that the Court's precedent should stand. It appeared that it was not whether the U.S. Supreme Court followed precedent or overruled it. It was not the method that seemed as important as the content of the decisions which were adjudged by observers to be consonant with their views or contrary to their views.

What was the follow-up to the Gideon case?

Following the Supreme Court's reversal of his conviction, Gideon was tried a second time. Though his difficult nature caused him to tangle with the trial counsel appointed this time for him, further investigation suggested that someone other than Gideon probably committed the burglary and in his second trial Gideon was found not guilty.

Twenty years after the decision in Gideon, Anthony Lewis concluded that the case indicated that the rights in the United States Constitution "are not self executing. They have to be fought for in every generation." Others also criticized the implementation of the decision arguing that state appointed lawyers were unable to provide adequate representation, that they presented merely the facade of counsel because of economic and time constraints. While the decision itself was moral, critics termed its practical result "Gideon's muted trumpet." The question of how poor the representation can be and still be adequate is a question which will be explored further in the chapter on professional conduct, for it is an issue that runs throughout much of the material on making the moral decision.

Forty years after Gideon, the National Association of Criminal Defense Lawyers argued that some public defenders had too many cases and two few resources. The NAACP Legal Defense Fund and the Georgia Indigent Defense Commission, and a Massachusetts district court judge, among others, found that the right to counsel was not being adequately provided and that the lack of public defenders was overwhelming courts. The judge explained that "I am faced with an intolerable choice—detaining people who have not been proven guilty and who have not had a fair chance to argue their side—or releasing people whom the prosecutor convincingly argues are both guilty and dangerous." And *The New York Times* argued that every defendant ought to be entitled to appointed counsel for his first appeal as well as for his initial trial.

How should justices interpret the U.S. Constitution?

Beyond the more immediate matter of counsel for indigent defendants in criminal cases, Gideon v. Wainwright implicitly focused on the great controversy surrounding the role of the U.S. Supreme Court and the accompanying question of nominees to that Court. One's personal answer to the question, "Who should be on the Supreme Court?" reflects one's notion of how the Supreme Court should decide cases and therefore who should be on it.

Two major interpretive possibilities have been loosely defined in the phrases original intent and evolving standards. The central issue was one of interpretation of the U.S. (or of another) Constitution: Should Justices find and apply the original intent of the Founders, as modified through procedures prescribed by them, or should Justices respect later, evolving or evolved views which may be quite different from what the Founders or legislatures did? Books by Raoul Berger and Ronald Dworkin advocated the two sides of this controversy, and the nominations of Robert Bork and David Souter some time ago, and the more recent nominations of now Chief Justice John Roberts and Associate Justice Samuel Alito showed the issue in its important practical consequences. The Senate rejected Judge Bork and confirmed Judges Souter, Roberts, and Alito to the U.S. Supreme Court.

What is the originalist view?

Raoul Berger argued that the U.S. Supreme Court has actually usurped power from the legislature and revised the Constitution under the disguise of interpreting it, especially where the Fourteenth Amendment was at issue. He disapproved strongly of this process and said that those who approved of the various Court decisions, especially as they applied to rights and liberty, considered the Court to be acting in an exemplary way when it exercised its power to interpret the Constitution and interpreted it in conformity with their deeply held views, often deciding to fill what he termed a "moral void." He subtitled his book, "The transformation of the 14th Amendment," and considered two essential questions. The first question was historical. What did the words of the Constitution mean to the original framers? The second question was moral. Should the original intentions of those framers be binding today? He answered the second question in the affirmative and he engaged in extensive historical research to illuminate the first question. He concluded by stating that "Power in the service of moral imperatives must not rest on a sham." He claimed that it would be better, for example, for school segregation to have continued longer than for the judiciary's attempt to legislate the issue. Berger emphasized that the Constitution excluded the judiciary from policy making. He sharply rejected the position revealed in his title and outlined in his book, *Government by Judiciary*.

Berger argued for judicial restraint. He declared that Supreme Court Justices should decide according to the original intent of the Framers, engaging in strict interpretation, and deferring to the legislature. He believed in majoritarian rule with the judiciary only serving to restrain the legislature in instances where they significantly departed from the Framers' intent. In essence, Berger took the philosophical view of Bentham and Mill and invoked the utilitarian principle which exalted the greatest happiness of the greatest number as evidenced by the legislators who, by their winning and taking office, represented the majority of the people.

What is the evolving standards view?

Ronald Dworkin held a directly opposing view of interpreting the U.S. Constitution. He called it a "liberal theory of laws." He was not concerned with the original intent of the framers as examined by Berger. Instead Dworkin argued for the application of an evolved constitutional standard to today's moral problems in an effort to fill the void left by legislatures, who did not act in accord with Dworkin's view of the moral rights and wrongs inherent in the framers' Constitution. He wrote, "Our Constitutional system rests on a particular moral theory, namely, that men have moral rights against the state." He believed that the U.S. Supreme Court "must be an activist court, in the sense that it must be prepared to frame and answer questions of political morality."

Dworkin's assessment of Court decisions depended on his view of the correctness of their result in achieving liberal goals of protecting people from the State rather than on the process of their decision. Making the moral decision meant to him interpreting the Constitution, with contemporary adaptations, in such a way that this liberal ideal (or those ideals) could be reached. This idea was encapsulated in the title of his book, *Taking Rights Seriously*.

Dworkin argued for a certain kind of judicial activism. Supreme Court Justices, he maintained, should decide in accord with evolving standards of decency, engaging in liberal construction, leading or contradicting the legislature. He believed in minority rights as a paramount concern of the judiciary as it worked to advance the rights of those different from the majority and who were therefore ignored or harmed by the legislative majoritarian rule. In essence, Dworkin shared the philosophical view of Immanuel Kant and John Rawls and invoked the principle of rights which exalts the importance of conferring rights on all, often through Courts, regardless of what most might want as evidenced by Legislatures who represented the majority of the people. In matters where the majority, and he and his adherents disagreed, Dworkin argued for declining to listen to the majority. Courts, he argued, as did Anthony Lewis, must take the lead.

In 2007, Dworkin began his review of what he termed the Supreme Court phalanx by saying: "The revolution that many commentators predicted when President Bush appointed two ultra-right-wing Supreme Court justices is proceeding with breathtaking impatience, and it is a revolution Jacobin in its disdain for tradition and precedent." He scorned the basis on which they rested their legal and moral decision making: "It seems guided by no judicial or political principle at all, but only by partisan, cultural, and perhaps religious allegiance." And he concluded with a harshly worded assessment of what he termed "the continuing subversion of the American Constitution. The worst is yet to come."

In 2007, Dworkin received the Holberg International Memorial Prize which recognized his scholarly achievement. He was described as "probably the most influential figure in contemporary Anglo-American legal theory." He argued that legal decisions should be guided by basic moral principles. As an example, he argued that racial quotas did not violate the rights of white applicants.

What is Borking?

Robert Bork, who was nominated in 1987 to fill a seat on the U.S. Supreme Court, but then not confirmed by the Senate, has been memorialized through a term, Borking, which applies to the process used to defeat him. The President of the liberal group People for the American Way contributed the verb (it meant to demonize a judicial nominee to block his nomination) as he blocked Bork's nomination and then tried to block the nomination of a black conservative, Clarence Thomas, to the U.S. Supreme Court. Conservatives also used the technique to block the nominations of a black liberal, Lani Guinier, to a Justice Department post, calling her a "quota queen." Liberals used it to block the nomination of a conservative Hispanic, Miguel Estrada, to an appellate federal court, calling him "too much of an ideologue to be an appeals court judge;" and of an African-American conservative justice on the California Supreme Court, Janice Rogers Brown, to the U.S. Supreme Court, calling her among the very worst judicial nominees. The technique was used to block the nomination, even to an obscure post on the board of the U.S. Institute of Peace, of a Mid-east Harvard scholar, Daniel Pipes, who was called a racist and a bigot because he favored profiling young Arab men though he made clear his view that radical Islam, not Islam itself, was the threat.

During all those and subsequent confirmations, whether to the Supreme Court or to other positions, that term reflected concern and practice among adherents to the very different ways of interpreting the Constitution or of assessing the roles of the Courts in relation to the Judiciary, or to the varying decisions of those who were very conservative or very liberal.

The term originated as, during his confirmation hearing to replace Justice Powell, Judge Bork engaged in a spirited exchange with Senators, and defended his record, writings, and comments. Opponents pictured him as indifferent or hostile to individual rights and questioned his views on the expansion or contraction of individual rights, on who should decide, and what the standards of decision should be. Both his knowledge and his ideology were examined and the latter caused his failure to achieve confirmation as a Supreme Court Justice. He condemned civil rights decisions; he wanted to overturn decisions and narrow the Fourteenth Amendment. He was both condemned and praised as a constitutional fundamentalist. One news commentator at the time wondered at Judge Bork's responses in the confirmation hearings: "He wants to be confirmed, doesn't he?"

What caused the Senate to reject his nomination?

In his book on the failure of the confirmation of Robert Bork to the Supreme Court, Ethan Bronner examined Bork's strict constructionist judicial philosophy, and the attacks on that philosophy made by liberal senators and groups like People for the American Way, the American Civil Liberties Union, and Common Cause. Bork believed the Constitution should be interpreted in accord with the original intent of the Framers and not in accord with today's approaches to the resolution of moral problems. Bronner argued that that view and a number of factors prevented Bork's confirmation to the Supreme Court. These included Bork's inability to clearly state his views and to succinctly respond to challenges; his inconsistencies and attempted revisions of some of his views as presented in his writings and talks, seemingly in an effort to placate his most severe critics in the Senate; and the American Bar Associations' split vote on whether he was qualified for the U.S. Supreme Court (four of fourteen found him "not qualified") were influential. Bronner subtitled his book "How the Bork nomination shook America" and viewed the struggle as a *Battle for Justice*.

In his own book, *The Tempting of America*, Robert Bork detailed his constitutional philosophy of original understanding and argued for strict construction of the Constitution even on civil rights, and the issue of privacy, and the status of women. He argued later in the book that his views were distorted in the Senate hearings. But he did not seem to understand the part his own manner, character, and even appearance played in his rejection. Bork seemed to imply during the Senate hearings that he had actually changed his mind on some issues. The change seemed opportunistic, not principled. Further, his manner and approach, perhaps with his ideas, failed to ignite opposition to the government by judiciary he deplored. He lost.

What, almost two decades later, did he say about the Constitution and its interpretation?

In January 2006, Robert Bork contributed his list of the five top books on the U.S. Constitution, with brief comments on each book, to the opinion page of the *Wall Street Journal*. First on his list was *The Federalist* by Hamilton, Madison, and Jay, and though he praised their effort, he lamented that they "failed to anticipate the political power that a judiciary entrusted with the Constitution would seize." Next was Supreme Court Justice and Harvard Law professor Joseph Story's *Commentaries* (1883) in which Story rejected judicial activism. Bork lamented the modern Court's notion of elasticity. Third was Alexander Bickel's *The Least Dangerous Branch* in which the author defended non-originalism. While the United States was founded on majoritarian principles, Bickel argued that the Court should apply the "evolving morality of our tradition." Bork praised the honesty of the argument while disagreeing with the view. The fourth book, *The Rise of Modern Judicial Review* by Christopher Wolfe, criticized the Court's activism and its defenders, a view with which Bork agreed. And the final book on his list, Philip Hamburger's *Separation of Church and State*, detailed what Bork termed "the modern era of judicial hostility to organized religion and its symbols in the public square." Bork considered that contrary to the Framers' prohibition of the establishment of religion. Bork retained his strong support for the originalist view, in his review of books about the Constitution and the Supreme Court and in his own edited book, *A Country I Do Not Recognize: The legal assault on American values.*

What did Clarence Thomas say was the reason for his Borking?

In his autobiographical book, *My Grandfather's Son*, Justice Clarence Thomas argued that the Anita Hill testimony before the Senate committee considering his nomination to the Supreme Court, while ostensibly about the subject of sexual harassment, was actually about the subtext of abortion. He contended that she was used by pro-choice forces in an attempt to derail his nomination because of their fear of his pro-life position. They worried that he would vote to overturn Roe v. Wade, and so used the material Anita Hill thought she had submitted confidentially when it appeared he would be confirmed. She then was thrust before the cameras and the nation to state her charge that he had sexually harassed her some ten years before. Meeting the strong accusations, Thomas mounted an equally strong counter-offensive. He reiterated his charge during the hearings that his treatment by the Committee amounted to a "high-tech lynching" of an "uppity black" who dared to differ from the so-called black, liberal, pro-choice view of those who attacked.

Even years after he won confirmation, one of Clarence Thomas' former Supreme Court clerks assessed the media's continuing reaction to him, especially re-occasioned by the publication of his memoir. She declared that it was not his ideas that brought forth the anger but "that he dares to contradict their own notions of who he should be, what he should think, and what kind of life he should lead. Indeed, the coverage at issue is not composed of arguments against the ideas expressed in the book but of the classic argumentum ad hominem—'arguments against the man.' As the book shows, the thread that weaves through all the diverse experiences in the justice's life—… and now to originalist jurist—is his insistence on independence. During all these times of his life, he refused to be controlled by the relevant establishment or indeed by any person."

What is a stealth nominee to the U.S. Supreme Court?

When liberal Justice William Brennan announced his retirement from the Supreme Court, President Bush nominated putative conservative David Souter, a New Hampshire judge, about whom very little was known because he had not commented widely as Judge Bork had. Nonetheless liberal groups were upset and hoped to oppose the nomination. Preceding the hearing Judge Souter prepared extensively. He set out to prove he was not Bork. At the hearings, he appeared to be a pragmatic moderate, later calling himself a moderate conservative, though he refused to define liberty or privacy, or to speak directly to the issue of abortion. At the least, he showed the capacity to participate effectively with his questioners. Whatever his views on many of the central issues confronting society, he showed he was confirmable, he was not Bork.

Judge Souter responded to questions concerning a right to privacy by saying, "I believe that the due process clause of the 14th Amendment does recognize and does protect an unenumerated right of privacy." His comment satisfied liberals to some extent, as Judge Bork had not, but worried conservatives, as again Judge Bork had not. But Judge Bork lost his fight and was not confirmed. Conservatives hoped and liberals feared that Souter's statements on the path to confirmation might not actually reflect his actions once on the Supreme Court. The fear of liberals concerning Judge Souter involved his possible future role in solidifying an anti-civil rights, anti-privacy majority on the U.S. Supreme Court. His lack of a written record and his quiet, thoughtful approach and simple values carried him through, however.

Judge Bork supported Judge Souter's refusal to cast judging in terms of his own moral and political leanings. Bork still opposed a Constitutional right of privacy which he argued was invented in Griswold v. Connecticut to render unconstitutional Connecticut's anti-contraception statute, and which is vague, not mentioned in the Constitution and essentially a blank slate for the Justices to fill as they exercise powers which Bork felt must be reserved under our government for legislatures.

A final point: Judge Bork objected to the blank slate view of the Constitution. He wanted clear indication of the Framers' original intent so judges could follow it. Yet Judge Souter presented to the Senate a virtual blank slate of views. They wanted to know his intent and his message was clear. Wait and see. And waiting, they did see that he was a generally liberal voice on the Court. In fact, a 2007 book by Jeffrey Toobin reported that Justice David Souter was so shattered by the decision of the Supreme Court in Bush v. Gore allowing Bush to assume the presidency that he both considered resigning and wept when he thought of that case. His was clearly a nomination that, largely because of its stealth, turned out much differently from what those who nominated him had in mind at the outset.

Were some nominees non-stealth candidates and nonetheless confirmed?

Yes, some nominees in the past been non-stealth candidates and nonetheless confirmed. A liberal attorney Ruth Bader Ginsburg, who served as the general counsel and member of the national board of directors of the American Civil Liberties Union and who refused to answer any questions about her judicial philosophy, was overwhelmingly confirmed by a 96-3 vote; yes, a conservative judge, Antonin Scalia, was overwhelmingly confirmed by a vote of 98-0. Either those voting for confirmation assumed that the personal background and views of the candidates would not decisively determine their interpretation of the Constitution, or they simply decided that qualification of candidates by education, temperament, standing in the legal and other communities, and so forth ought to be more important than judicial philosophy or religion or philosophy in general. That was not the case with Robert Bork who had given his judicial philosophy, over and over, and who was not confirmed by the Senate.

Has stealth increased?

With increasing charges of activism leveled against both liberal and conservative judges, the importance of stealth on the major roiling issues, such as abortion, has become increasingly important. More recent nominees, who have not had an extensive record of positions taken on the key methods of interpreting the Constitution, and who wanted to be confirmed, side-stepped direct answers to Senatorial questions about precedents, and stare decisis, and judicial philosophy, and other matters which would lead Senators to vote for or against them based on their already-made-up minds about abortion, the role of the Supreme Court, the relation between legislatures and courts, and similar topics.

What are four major approaches to making moral decisions concerning law and ethics?

Having considered Hunter Lewis' six methods of moral reasoning, and the two major methods of Constitutional interpretation, we conclude this section by examining at least four approaches that may be taken to making moral decisions concerning material from law and ethics. One of these can be called the legal approach; others are the social science, the philosophical, and the religious approaches. While there are obvious overlaps in these approaches, it is helpful to understand the differences among them as well as the similarities.

What is the legal approach?

The 1963 case of Gideon v. Wainwright, already discussed, illustrated the first approach, the legal approach. The U.S. Supreme Court took Gideon's case and overruled Betts v. Brady. In writing the Opinion of the Court, Justice Black asserted, "We accept Betts v. Brady's assumption ... that a provision of the Bill of Rights which is 'fundamental and essential to fair trial' is made obligatory upon the states by the Fourteenth Amendment. We think the Court in Betts was wrong, however, in concluding that the Sixth Amendment's guarantee of counsel is not one of these fundamental rights. Twenty three states, as friends of the Court, argue that Betts was an 'anachronism when handed down' and that it should now be overruled. We agree. The judgment is reversed and the cause is remanded to the Supreme Court of Florida for action not inconsistent with this opinion."

Commenting on the role of the U.S. Supreme Court, Anthony Lewis wrote in *Gideon's Trumpet:* "The Court's function is not to reflect mass ideas but to lead enlightened opinion, to educate. At its best the Court is a great teacher, illuminating issues and then drawing support for further steps from the more sensitive public attitudes it has helped to create."

The first of these approaches, the legal approach, relied on the U.S. Constitution; judicially reviewed or reexamined causes; usually followed stare decisis by adhering to precedents; acknowledged federalism; proceeded through adversarial arguments; appealed to reason and logic and the authority of prior cases; and included written briefs and written opinions. The legal approach involved the statutes rendered by legislatures as well as their interpretation by the judiciary. Many controversies arose concerning the legal approach. Among them were the following. Which method ought to guide interpretation, seeking the original intent or invoking the evolving standards? Which branch ought to be the guardian of moral decision making, the legislature or the judiciary? To what extent ought precedent to be adhered to, and when can it or should it be overruled? Should the focus of interpretation be on the United States as a whole or on the individual states, or even on laws outside the United States? What kind of evidence beyond the law should be used and from where, from social science, from philosophy, from religion, or from elsewhere?

What is the social science approach?

In arguing "The case for abolition" of so-called *Victimless Crimes*, sociologist Schur relied on social science evidence, as so many others did, to detail the costs of criminalizing drug use, prostitution, gambling, homosexuality, and all "crimes without victims;" the costs of enforcement; the economic effects of making wanted goods and services illegal and harder to get; the creation of large numbers of criminals; and the corruption and disrespect for the law which resulted from the enormous discretion vested in the police when full enforcement was recognized to be impossible and public opinion was highly ambivalent with respect to the laws. Balancing these costs against the benefit of making the law reflected a particular moral view to discourage certain behavior considered immoral, Schur argued for the decriminalization of these victimless crimes.

Concluding, he wrote: "To marshal empirical evidence as has been done here is not to argue for extreme utilitarianism in which it is assumed that some kind of quantitative calculation can produce authoritative answers to complex moral questions. In the absence of universal moral consensus, assessments of evidence and weighings of alternatives will necessarily entail reference to particular value hierarchies."

This second approach, the social science approach, relied on sociological, psychological and other social science evidence. It often used a cost/benefit paradigm, tended to be politically liberal as opposed to politically conservative in its orientation, and focused on the world as it is or as secular humanists say it should be rather than as traditional religions say it should be.

What is the philosophical approach?

In his argument in *Victimless Crimes,* the philosopher Bedau wrote: "Society and government should allow persons to engage in whatever conduct they want to, no matter how deviant or abnormal it may be, so long as (a) they know what they are doing, (b) they consent to it, and (c) no one at least no one other than the participants is harmed by it." And he said: "The philosophical source of this important principle is to be found in the famous essay *On Liberty* written by John Stuart Mill over a century ago." Bedau called it "liberalism" and said that it "is clear from Mill's argument's context that he believes there is a strong presumption in favor of the finality of any adult person's judgment about what he does and does not like, want, or find harmful." He then concluded, "Mill's liberalism gives us a moral basis as valid in our day as it was in his for reforming the criminal code."

This third approach, the philosophical approach, started with a moral philosophy, such as classical liberalism, and argued based on that philosophy; or it started with a philosopher, such as Immanuel Kant or John Rawls or John Stuart Mill, and applied his philosophical writings to situations in the world. It often proceeded by analogy, carried arguments to their extremes, and relied on intuition, reflection, or personal experience.

What is the religious approach?

The fourth approach is the religious approach. This fourth approach started with a religious tradition, such as Judaism or Christianity or Islam, perhaps with a more specific religion, such as Roman Catholicism or Christian Science or Evangelical Christianity, or Unitarianism and argued based on the doctrines of that religious practice. Or it started with a religious leader such as Jesus, Muhammed, the Rev. Billy Graham, the Pope, Mary Baker Eddy, or others and applies their moral teachings. This approach proceeded by reference to religious texts, to divine communications, and to authority in taking moral stands. Different religions emphasized different moral issues and had varying views concerning them.

All four of these approaches to making the moral decision have found strong support, and while many reached similar conclusions, their differences were also striking. Were the law not involved, each approach would simply have its adherents and detractors. Because the law was involved in the ethical questions which follow, some one or more of the approaches became embedded in the law and said what society considered the moral decision to be.

What moral issues does this book examine?

This book examines four basic life-and-death moral issues. They are abortion, care of children, capital punishment, and the right to die. And then it examines four administrative issues. They are affirmative action, professional conduct, sexual conduct, and privacy.

Having provided an overview of the broad ranging problems of morality and the law, we now turn to a discussion of the moral and legal issues regarding the abortion question.

Basic Issues

3

Abortion

What is the legal and moral problem?

Abortion is in many ways a legal and moral problem that contains within it the various questions which this book addresses. Among the major questions are these. Is the U.S. Constitution a proper focus for arguments concerning abortion? Are Supreme Court Justices, whose training is in law, not in theology or philosophy or related disciplines, the ones who should be making these kinds of decisions? Or are legislators, responding to the various mandates of their constituents, however those voters arrive at their decisions, the ones who should be making these decisions? Or should such decisions be left to the individual primarily affected, with whatever assistance she might want to draw upon? Further questions arise. What is the relation between secular moral views and religious (especially denominational) views? How can two absolute, opposed views, the so-called pro-choice and the pro-life positions, each claimed to be the moral one by advocates for that view, ever be reconciled? Short of reconciliation, how can the clash between those opposed views be resolved, so that some direction is clear?

Beyond an attempt to reconcile the views, which view will predominate and how will it be decided? And how do the opposing views consider all the various concepts to actually mean: life, quality of life, personhood, viability, privacy, moral decision making, law?

More specifically, these overall concepts raise further questions. When does human life begin? When does personhood begin? What are the moral rights of the woman who is carrying the fetus? What are the moral rights of the fetus? How are they to be balanced? What if the fetus can survive outside the womb at or just after conception? Does the fact that the Fourteenth Amendment to the United States Constitution protects persons, not life, affect the issues? To what extent does or should our concept of person include both psychological and physical state? If our concept of person should be inclusive, at what point in the devel-

41

oping fetus is there a united, functioning body and mind? Who ought to decide when life begins: doctors, Congress, the Court, or clerics? How can one reconcile varying religious views concerning abortion? Should there be a vote on the abortion issue? Ought the majority view to prevail? And to what extent would minority rights be protected against the majority in such a vote?

There are many answers to the questions raised by the abortion issue. Neither the religious nor the political answer is unitary. Nor is there one legal or philosophical answer. But there are arguments. We begin each moral problem with legal analysis which contains within it ethical considerations. A court approaches the issues and argues by analogy, through religious examples or concepts, using declarative statements, by referring to precedents or other cases, in its attempt to make the moral and legal decision. Thus, in the topic of abortion, we examine the landmark case of Roe v. Wade and more recent comments on it.

What did the U.S. Supreme Court case of Roe v. Wade decide?

In 1973, Roe v. Wade, by a vote of 6 to 3, held that the Texas statutes criminalizing abortion were unconstitutional. Justice Blackmun began his majority opinion by acknowledging "our awareness of the sensitive and emotional nature of the abortion controversy, of the vigorous opposing views, even among physicians, and of the deep and seemingly absolute convictions that the subject inspires. One's philosophy, one's experiences, one's exposure to the raw edges of human existence, one's religious training, one's attitudes toward life and family and their values, and the moral standards one establishes and seeks to observe, are all likely to influence and to color one's thinking and conclusions about abortion. In addition, population growth, pollution, poverty, and racial overtones tend to complicate and not to simplify the problem. Our task, of course, is to resolve the issue by constitutional measurement, free of emotion and of predilection. We seek earnestly to do this, and, because we do, we have inquired into, and in this opinion, place some emphasis upon, medical and medical/legal history and what that history reveals about man's attitudes toward the abortion procedure over the centuries."

The case involved a single pregnant Texas woman, given the name Jane Roe for the case to protect her privacy. She (meaning, of course, her lawyers) "claimed that the Texas Statutes were unconstitutionally vague and that they abridged her right of personal privacy, protected by the First, Fourth, Fifth, Ninth, and Fourteenth Amendments." She expanded her complaint to include all other women in similar situations.

In deciding the case, the majority acknowledged that "The Constitution does not explicitly mention any right of privacy." Nonetheless, it said that "In varying contexts, the Court or individual Justices have, indeed, found at least the roots of that right in the First Amendment, in the Fourth and Fifth Amendment, in the penumbras of the Bill of Rights in the Ninth Amendment, or in the concept of liberty guaranteed by the first section of the Fourteenth Amendment."

The majority concluded that "This right of privacy is broad enough to encompass a woman's decision whether or not to terminate her pregnancy." Further it concluded that a fetus was not a person as that term was used in the U.S. Constitution. "In short, the unborn have never been recognized in the law as persons in the whole sense."

Dividing the pregnancy into trimesters, the Court ruled that during the first, the woman's physician should provide the medical judgment; during the second, the State might regulate the procedure to protect the mother's health; and during the third, following viability, the State might even make abortion illegal.

What was said in dissenting to the ruling in Roe v. Wade?

In his dissenting opinion, Justice White wrote: "At the heart of the controversy in these cases are those recurring pregnancies that pose no danger whatsoever to the life or health of the mother but are, nevertheless, unwanted for any one or more of a variety of reasons: convenience, family planning, economics, dislike of children, the embarrassment of illegitimacy, etc. The common claim before us is that for any one of such reasons, or for no reason at all, and without asserting or claiming any threat to life or health, any woman is entitled to an abortion at her request if she is able to find a medical advisor willing to undertake the procedure." During the period prior to the time the fetus becomes viable, Justice White continued by saying that the majority declared that "the Constitution of the United States values the convenience, whim, or caprice of the pregnant woman more than the life of the fetus"

He said he dissented because he found "nothing in the language or history of the Constitution to support the Court's judgments. The Court simply fashions and announces a new constitutional right for pregnant women and with scarcely any reason or authority for its action invests the right with sufficient substance to override most existing state abortion statutes. The upshot is that the people and the legislatures of the 50 States are constitutionally disentitled to weigh the relative importance of the continued existence and development of the fetus, on the one hand, against a spectrum of possible impacts on the mother, on the other hand. As an exercise of raw judicial power, the Court perhaps has authority to do what it does today; but in my view its judgment is an improvident and extravagant exercise of the power of judicial review that the Constitution extends to this Court. The Court apparently values the convenience of the pregnant woman more than the continued existence and development of the life or potential life that she carries. Whether or not I might agree with the marshalling of values, I can in no event join the Court's judgment because I find no constitutional warrant for imposing such an order of priorities on the people and legislatures of the States. In a sensitive area such as this, involving as it does issues over which reasonable men may easily and heatedly differ, I cannot accept the Court's exercise of its clear power of choice by interposing a constitutional barrier to state efforts to protect human life and by investing women and doctors with the constitutionally protected right to exterminate it. This issue, for the most part, should be left with the people and to the political processes the people have devised to govern their affairs."

Despite saying that he might or not, did one dissenting Justice appear to disagree with the marshalling of values by the majority?

From his strong words it appeared evident that Justice White, though he said he might or might not agree, did disagree with valuing the mother more than the fetus. What the source of his disagreement was might be subject to speculation. It could have been the authority of his Roman Catholic religion, and its stance against abortion, which he could not or decided not to cite directly as the source of his view. It could have been some emotional antipathy to what he saw as the fickleness of women, catering to what he called their own convenience, whim, or caprice. It could have been some personal experience which occasioned a strong comment from him. Or perhaps something else. In any event, any disclaimer often signals the reader to explore more carefully the comments it disclaims.

What opposing views of the role of the judiciary in making a moral decision about abortion did *Roe v. Wade* present?

In Roe v. Wade the opinion of a majority of the U.S. Supreme Court relied on a rights-oriented concept of privacy in overturning the legislature's statute. It took seriously the woman's wish to terminate her pregnancy and it asserted the primacy of the judiciary in making the moral decision as it found unconstitutional the dominant view of the legislators who had enacted the law in question. The dissent relied on a utilitarian-oriented concept as it asserted the primacy of the legislature by giving deference to their dominant view of safeguarding the fetus despite the woman's wish. The two competing approaches toward Constitutional interpretation, the liberal finding in the "penumbras" of the Constitution the reasons to make an unprecedented decision, and the conservative dismissing the decision as an exercise of "raw judicial power" were explicitly advocated by majority and dissenting opinions.

While the constitutional right to an abortion remained preserved, some of the subsequent decisions narrowed it somewhat and liberals remained concerned that more conservative appointments to the Supreme Court would narrow it further or even overturn it. Thus the two views present in Roe v. Wade continue to inform Constitutional interpretation and the controversy surrounding it and the Justices who practice each of them.

What did the real Jane Roe say when she acknowledged her identity?

Norma McCorvey was pregnant when she met the lawyers who were looking for a pregnant woman to become a Jane Roe in an attempt to overturn state abortion laws. That was in 1970. The case was not decided by the U.S. Supreme Court until 1973. She said she did not realize how long the case would take through the legal system; that she never did have an abortion; that she had given her baby girl up for adoption; that she felt used by the attorneys who had befriended her and then abandoned her once the case was decided; that she had not had stability in her life; and that, when she announced she was Jane Roe, the supporters of abortion basically rejected her because she did not fit their idea of a role model.

Because Ms. McCorvey had her child out of wedlock; because she lied when seeking an abortion saying falsely that it was the result of her being raped; because she cooperated with attorneys to become a test case concerning the abortion stat-utes, pro-life advocates viewed her as immoral when she first came forth and then wrote her pro-choice book *I Am Roe*. Pro-choice advocates initially viewed her as a heroine and as a representative of women in turmoil who need to have the option of legal abortion, though she did not fit their view of the moral woman.

Why did the real Jane Roe change her position on abortion?

Ms. McCorvey was strongly pro-choice and working at a women's center when Operation Rescue moved in next door. Initially, she was hostile toward them. But then the Rev. Phillip Benham, its national director, became increasingly friendly with her when she regularly went outside to smoke. He treated her well, discussed Christianity with her, and gradually she changed her position to pro-life. She was baptized by him in 1995 in a nationally televised event.

The attitudes of the pro-choice and pro-life advocates toward her changed when Norma McCorvey shifted her view. She said she felt belittled and scorned by the pro-choice advocates because of her rough background. She was not their type of person to be the symbol of a woman's right to choose. She found comfort, however, with a pro-life minister, and other members of the pro-life movement. Baptized by him, she said that she had changed her mind, though she still felt that a woman had a right to choose in limited circumstances.

How moral was Jane Roe's attorney in the landmark case?

When Norma McCorvey met Sarah Weddington, who became one of her attor-neys in the landmark case, she had asked Ms. Weddington how she could obtain an abortion. Ms. Weddington told her she did not know. Subsequently in her own autobiography, Ms. Weddington revealed that she had gone to Mexico to have an abortion. Ms. McCorvey said she felt betrayed. It can be said that Sarah Weddington did not make the moral decision. Recall the appellate attorney's effort in the Gideon case to make the moral decision by determining whether Gideon fell within an exception which would have made him eligible for a court-provided attorney. If he had fit an exception, then the case could not go forward and the opportunity to overturn Betts v. Brady would be lost at that time. In that case, the attorney made the moral decision to investigate and, in so doing, discovered that Gideon did not fit one of the exceptions.

In the case of Ms. McCorvey, on the other hand, because the attorney needed a pregnant woman, it appeared that she wanted to maintain her pregnancy for the utilitarian purpose of helping other women who wanted abortions. In other words, Ms. Weddington appeared not to have been rights-oriented as far as Ms. McCorvey was concerned. Although Ms. Weddington said that she could not have directed Ms. McCorvey toward an abortion because that was illegal, many considered Weddington's actions to be immoral in that they used an individual in a utilitarian way without regard for that woman herself. She was used solely as a means to an end, not treated as an individual in her own right. It was reported in 2003 that Sarah Weddington said then that she would rather have picked a different plaintiff who would have represented the matter better. In a sense, Norma McCorvey did not abide by what might be termed a form of stare decisis. She overruled her earlier pro-choice view and became strongly pro-life.

What about adoption as an alternative to abortion?

Norma McCorvey, the Jane Roe of Roe v. Wade, never did have an abortion. It took over three years for her case to be resolved by the U.S. Supreme Court and by that time she had given birth and given her baby up for adoption. When she came forth later to identify herself, she said that she regretted that decision to adopt out her infant.

Her reaction to adoption was an especially influential but often little discussed factor in a woman's choice of abortion. It has been suggested that the fear of guilt at giving up the child for adoption may propel the woman toward abortion, that for many women it is not morally acceptable to give up a baby for adoption. Women make the moral decision to keep their children or the moral decision to seek abortion rather than adoption when they know that economic, personal or psychological circumstances will prevent their keeping their newborns. Recent changes in adoption laws making them more open may or may not impact these kinds of decisions.

What effect did Roe v. Wade continue to have on subsequent confirmations to the U.S. Supreme Court?

Although subsequent decisions of the U.S. Supreme Court served to narrow somewhat the ability of women to obtain abortions, as for example in the procedure opponents call partial-birth abortion, the case of Roe v. Wade maintained women's constitutional right to choose whether to have an abortion. As such, that decision remained controversial and important.

In the 1990 confirmation hearings of Judge David Souter to the U.S. Supreme Court, Planned Parenthood addressed six questions to him in an effort to determine whether he, as a Supreme Court Justice, would uphold the privacy principles formed in the 1965 Griswold v. Connecticut decision which forbid states from banning birth control and in the 1973 Roe v. Wade decision which permitted women to obtain abortions. Planned Parenthood asked the following questions. Does the Constitution protect any rights other than those specifically spelled out? Is the right to privacy a fundamental right equal to freedom of speech, religion, and the press or only a "liberty interest" subject to state regulation? Does the Constitution protect the right to privacy in matters of family life and reproduction, including the use of contraception? Does the state have a compelling interest in forcing a woman to continue pregnancy against her will? Does constitutional "personhood" exist from the moment of contraception? And subsequent Senate confirmation hearings have attempted to learn the views of nominees toward abortion.

But Souter and subsequent nominees did not specifically answer those questions. They tended to restate their respect for precedent and stare decisis, saying they would not prejudge matters but would take each case as it presented itself. Senators on both sides of the abortion issue could only attempt to predict what decisions each nominee would support by looking at the nominator, whatever they could find of the nominee's past record, and statements by others concerning the nominee.

More recent appointments to the U.S. Supreme Court of more conservative, restrained judges who tended to advocate deference to the legislature showed that a heretofore more evenly balanced liberal/conservative Court with one member, now retired, as a swing vote, might tip away from the rights-oriented view. As one Senator asked of nominees who had professed adherence to stare decisis, yet who said that some precedents which were bad or immoral had been wisely overruled, were there some precedents (as Roe v. Wade) that were what he called super-duper precedents, and therefore not overruleable. Time, of course, will tell.

Beyond precedent, as we will see in Bowers v. Hardwick and as we apparently can see in Roe v. Wade, advocacy of judicial restraint may also happen to fit the personal, religious, and secular morality of the judges. Justice White disapproved of abortion, as did Justice Scalia; Justice Burger abhorred homosexuality. It surely seemed easier for one to argue for deference to legislatures if they are legislating one's own personal morality.

What other approaches are there to the moral problem of abortion?

While the U.S. Supreme Court cases discuss privacy, personhood, whim and caprice, there are other approaches to making the moral decision concerning abortion. Among the most significant and influential of these are religious approaches.

Whatever courts decide, the Roman Catholic and some conservative or fundamental Protestant views were that the purpose of abortion is death and they argued that liberals who abhorred state condoned killing of the guilty in capital punishment nevertheless approved of abortion. Those who condemned abortion considered it to be governed by an ethics of convenience and argued that the legal language was clouded to cover the reality of fetus killing. They adhered to the pro-life view that personhood was an inborn and an inalienable right from the moment of conception. They considered the moral order clear, God-given, and said that courts should not alter that.

The Roman Catholic outlook was that the ban on abortion was absolute. Abortion was a sin and the violation of a human being's right to life. Making the moral decision required recognition that killing an innocent human was wrong. In fact, the Pope reiterated his view in September 2007 at a meeting of international organizations in Vienna saying that "The fundamental human right is the right to life itself." He went on to say that "This is true from the moment of conception until its natural end. Abortion, consequently, cannot be a human right. It is the very opposite." Right to life committees agreed. They argued that killing for utilitarian reasons was not morally acceptable.

Liberal Protestant and other churches, however, allowed their members greater variation as they made the moral decision concerning abortion. Some supported women's decisions concerning their own bodies; others liberally listed reasons for justifying abortion, reasons ranging from the physical or mental health or life of the mother to socioeconomic conditions of the family. Within the Jewish religion, the emphasis was on the welfare of the mother, which suggested a pro-choice orientation.

The variation in religious views and the split between Roman Catholic and fundamentalist Protestant religions, on the one hand, and other major religions' views, on the other hand, was made clear in a statement by the Coalition for Abortion Rights of Massachusetts which included the leaders of many Protestant and Jewish organizations. They declared the Catholic position to be morally indefensible, and advocated legal abortion and the right of individuals to follow their own religious tradition in general and as it concerns abortion.

What are the implications of the view that life begins at conception?

For those who considered that life began at conception, and the presidential candidate John Kerry said that he did and yet supported a woman's right to choose an abortion, the implications of the view were many. Carrying the matter of when life begins to its logical conclusion, some would say to extremes, suggested a number of changes. And carrying a matter to an extreme was a technique often used to assess a moral view. From that redefinition of the beginning of life, it would follow that the Census should require certificates of conception. Date-of-conception should replace date-of-birth. Taxes, political representation, Social Security, retirement benefits, driving age, and drinking age should all be refigured. Pregnant women would be liable to prosecution for administering alcohol to their under-age fetuses and bartenders for serving pregnant women and their fetus-minors. Pregnant women could be investigated for child abuse for smoking, eating poorly, drinking, forgoing adequate prenatal care, following poor hygiene techniques, exercising improperly. Pregnant, perhaps even fertile, women could be banned from work which posed potential risk to the unborn.

The impossibility of compromise underlay all arguments concerning abortion. In her book, *Abortion and the Politics of Motherhood*, Kristin Luker was pessimistic concerning any resolution to the conflicts surrounding abortion and considered class the most important variable in an individual's attitude regarding abortion. And Laurence Tribe subtitled his book, *Abortion*, "The clash of absolutes." While he attempted to present both sides of the abortion debate, he clearly sided with pro-choice advocates. And a compromise which allowed limited abortion still took the position of allowing abortion which pro-life advocates rejected.

The question really came down to a simple dichotomy. Was abortion simply a matter of private morality, a woman's choice aided by her doctor and others she consulted with, or was it a matter of public morality which demanded the legislature's or Court's choice imposed on women by law? Pro-choice advocates argued for the former, suggesting that some moral issues should be left to personal choice even though there were moral tradeoffs or costs in such a stance. Pro-life advocates argued for the latter.

How did an analogy help clarify the issue of abortion?

Judith Jarvis Thomson's famous example of her method of making the moral decision demonstrated a philosophical approach to moral decision making. She proceeded by analogy and extension to reach what she intuitively concluded was a moral decision.

In her article "A defense of abortion," Thomson elaborated at length on an example. She asked the reader to imagine that he or she awakes one morning with an unconscious famous dying violinist in bed, who has been hooked up to the circulatory system of the reader as the only means of sustaining the life of the violinist. The reader has not given permission for the procedure, and the violinist will die if unhooked from the reader, for the reader is, according to the example, the only individual who can sustain the life of the violinist.

Does the reader, she asked, have a moral obligation to stay hooked up to the violinist, briefly, for a longer time, or forever, in order to sustain the life of the violinist, or can the reader unhook him or herself, thus certainly causing the death of the violinist?

Thomson then analogized the situation of the reader and the violinist to the situation of the woman and the fetus, if the fetus were regarded as a person as the violinist is. If the fetus were not considered a person, then one need not go so far as the analogy with the violinist.

In the violinist analogy, Thomson extended her argument. She acknowledged that the violinist had been strapped to the reader without the latter's permission. Pursuing the related case of the pregnant woman, she raised the case of a woman who voluntarily had intercourse, and became pregnant. Would this not be tantamount to the reader's giving permission for the violinist to be strapped to her and then changing mind and reneging on the offer? Under those circumstances, ought the reader to be allowed to unhook the violinist?

Thomson then revised the violinist story to ask what should happen if the violinist needed only a brief period of time hooked to the reader. Ought not there to be a moral imperative to the reader to let the violinist be so hooked up? What if that brief period corresponded to the time required for the fetus to grow and be delivered? Ought not the woman to be mandated to keep the fetus for the time involved?

Thomson concluded that while a person should allow the violinist to hook up, especially for a short time, the person need not do so. Such an action was not morally required. No one, in her view, was morally required to make great sacrifices, to be a "Good Samaritan." Only the "Minimally Decent Samaritan," she argued, was morally mandated, not the ideal "Splendid Samaritan."

In her conclusion, Thomson acknowledged that in her argument abortion would at times be prohibited and that the individual who wanted to have an abortion could not be guaranteed the death of the fetus. Thus, in the violinist example, the reader could ask that the violinist be unhooked, but should that violinist nevertheless live, the reader could not be guaranteed the death of that violinist.

While Thomson did not in her article attempt to fit her argument to the concepts of basic Christian ethics, utilitarian ethics, the categorical imperative, or any other standard of ethical inquiry, her analysis may well have incorporated the distinctive premises of major formal ethical systems, though her Samaritan example modified at least one such system. Her article reflected, as she stated, her "own view," but it may reflect more as well.

What were two other responses to the issue of abortion?

An extreme, illegal action and a linking of abortion with crime reduction were two other responses to the moral problem of abortion.

A man killed an abortion-clinic doctor, he said, as both a practical matter and as a symbolic act to save the lives of numbers of unborn babies. He was convicted and sentenced to death. He was unrepentant as he faced execution. According to news reports, he insisted that he would be forgiven by God for killing to save the unborn. He said "I expect a great reward in heaven." "I am looking forward to glory."

And, in their book *Freakonomics*, a Chicago and a Stanford economics professor found a link between legalized abortion and crime reduction. They contended that the drop in the U.S. crime rate in the 1990s was directly linked to legalized abortion in the 1970s. They claimed that statistical evidence proved that the pool of potential law-breakers was radically reduced because young, poor, minority women were able to terminate their pregnancies. This conclusion about the utility of abortion clearly raised controversy.

Could arguments about abortion be extended to infanticide?

Extrapolating premises of permitted abortion to logical extremes is yet another method with which we can scrutinize the abortion issue. In her essay, "On the moral and legal status of abortion," Mary Anne Warren extended Thomson's argument. Initially, Warren used her intuition to declare that a fetus was not a person. She concluded a discussion of Thomson's article by arguing that the fetus' resembling a person and the fetus' potential for becoming a person did not suggest that it had a right to life. Because of this, Warren contended, a woman's right to do what she wanted would always be superior to the rights of the fetus, "even a fully developed one." Warren went further. She pointed out that her argument seemed to justify infanticide as well as abortion.

Warren's argument seemed to justify infanticide, she claimed, because the just born infant was not significantly different from the fetus just before birth. Warren argued that the difference between the fetus and the just born infant was that the just born was no longer under the mother's control. While the just born was no more a person than the before born fetus, the mother's right to determine what happened to it was no longer as important. The infant, for example, could be put up for adoption. But, Warren concluded, her argument suggested that an unwanted or defective new born in a society which could not or did not want to care for it could be destroyed. Though Warren stated that many people might conclude that her extension of the argument was immoral, such killing was nevertheless permissible, according to her argument. But her concluding statement softened her seeming advocacy of infanticide. As long as there were people, Warren argued, who want such just borns preserved, not destroyed, that was reason enough to preserve them.

Based on his utilitarian philosophy, what view about abortion did a bioethicist hold?

A professor of bioethics at Princeton University, however, took a different view concerning infanticide. His was a utilitarian view. Peter Singer argued that to increase pleasure and to reduce pain parents should be allowed twenty-eight days after the birth of a severely disabled child to decide whether to kill it. He argued that newborns were not persons in any meaningful sense of the word and therefore could be killed if the balance of pain to them, their parents, and society outweighed their present and future pleasure. And a professor at the University of Colorado declared that it was morally permissible to kill a newborn because personhood did not begin at birth, as the newborn had no sense of self. But he limited the time period in which it could be done to perhaps a week. And a Harvard professor said he took the scientific view that because newborns are not persons in the full sense of the word, mothers who kill their newborns should not be judged as harshly as those who kill older persons.

4

Care of Children

What does care of children involve?

While some consider the fetus as a child, the care of children does not include here those unborn fetuses. Our word children here connotes the born, not the unborn, and not the just born which we have considered in the chapter on abortion. As such, this chapter does not continue with the topic of abortion, nor does it re-discuss the matter of infanticide. Obviously, those who advocated parental rights to kill their newborns saw those less-than-a-month-old newborns as something less than children. This chapter, on the other hand, will consider three types of cases of the lack of care of children, all the cases dealing with religion and all resulting in the death of the child. Two of the cases have reached United States courts; one has not.

The type of case which has not reached the courts is one involving those who use the religion of Islam to convince children to become suicide/homicide bombers. According to their fanatical religious views, they were preparing those children to be welcomed by their God into their heaven, much as the adult suicide/bombers were assured, it is said, that virgins would await them in heaven after their killing of innocents. In that sense, all of them were similar in one way to the killer of the abortion-clinic doctor. All were convinced that their religion both encouraged and rewarded their behavior, behavior that the law in the United States considered criminal. It seemed impossible to convince them otherwise. Regardless of its stand on the morality of abortion, the Roman Catholic Church condemned the killing of abortion-clinic doctors. The Church declared the acts to be immoral acts. The law declared them to be illegal acts.

Two types of cases which have reached the courts and are relevant to our discussion of the relation between law and ethics in the care of children involve Christian Science parents and Roman Catholic priests. The first involves the death of a child whose Christian Science parents sought religious rather than standard medical care. The second involves the sexually predatory behavior of some Roman Catholic priests that was allowed to continue over an extended period of time by the cover-up of those in the hierarchy above them.

What is the moral problem?

Without doubt the death of a child while in the care and custody of his parents raised a moral question when the parents decided not to rely on conventional medicine but instead to turn to alternative forms of healing. The parents engaged in moral decision making. The children were forced to abide by the parent's decision, lacking as they did, the capacity to seek the conventional or at least to make informed choices, which they could do if they lived to their maturity.

In an earlier case in Massachusetts, not the result of religious conviction but of a turn to New Age medicine, the parents of a three-year old boy rejected the advice of the Massachusetts General Hospital for chemotherapy and turned instead to an alternative treatment for their son's diagnosed leukemia. The boy died. His parents, who had been out of state, returned to Massachusetts where a judge found them guilty of criminal contempt for their defiance of the court mandate, but imposed no punishment other than a period of probation, concluding that they had already suffered enough because of the death of their child. Those who supported the judge's decision felt that both the parents and the courts had failed the boy, the parents because of their poor judgment, and the courts because they failed to remove the boy from physical custody of his parents. Those who objected to the decision felt that the parents directly contributed to the boy's death through their immoral decision to withhold accepted medical treatment and supply instead the unaccepted alternative treatment. But the boy's mother added another dimension to the matter. She said: "The drugs had a debilitating effect on his little life. We wanted quality time for what was left of his life." The doctor at the Massachusetts General Hospital countered by saying that chemotherapy at that time would have given the boy a fifty-fifty chance to be alive three years later, while without treatment he had no chance. A few years later the boy's parents became the parents of a baby girl. The boy's case raised the question of the extent to which his parents ought to have oversight as they raised their daughter. At that time, the boy's case seemed to present as clear a picture as possible of an accepted medical treatment and an unaccepted alternative course.

But in two subsequent cases, almost a decade later, parents who followed the Christian Science religion and sought advice from the Church concerning their use of spiritual healing through alternative prayerful treatment for a daughter in one case and a son in the other, both of whom died, were found guilty of involuntary manslaughter.

What was the "crime" of Dorothy Sheridan?

Leo Damore wrote in his book *The "Crime" of Dorothy Sheridan* about a mother who, in 1967, relied on her Christian Science faith in prayer rather than on medicine when her daughter became ill. When the five year old girl died, the mother was charged with and convicted of involuntary manslaughter for her failure to provide proper physical care for her child. She had criminally violated the child neglect law.

In 1971, the Christian Science Church, headquartered in Boston, persuaded the Massachusetts legislature to pass a religious exemption to that child neglect law.

Who was responsible for Robyn Twitchell's death?

In 1986, two year old Robyn Twitchell died from what later turned out was an undiagnosed bowel obstruction. Though his parents relied on a religious exemption to the statute on child neglect which the Christian Science Church spokesperson had maintained meant that they did not have to seek medical care, they were charged and convicted in 1990, and sentenced to ten years' probation after a jury found them guilty of manslaughter. Subsequently the legislature repealed the statute to which the religious exemption was added.

What questions were raised by Robyn Twitchell's death?

Robyn Twitchell's parents, like Dorothy Sheridan, relied on an established religion's form of treatment for their son. The case raised many questions. Did the Twitchell's make a moral decision because they relied on religion and on the official spokesperson and a church manual for that religion? What is the relation between religion and morality? Can one be a moral person and rely on a moral religion and yet make an immoral decision? What is the relation between legal decision making and moral decision making?

Additional questions included these. How were the rights of the parents and of the children and of the state to be balanced? What did the parental right to practice their religion as they chose confer on them in terms of their care for their children? What should happen if the child died as a result of the parental practice of their religion? Further, and more specifically, what was the moral course of action for parents with a seriously ill child? And what ought the response of the law to be, while the child was alive, and after he has died? What was the relation between the religious, the moral, and the legal courses of action?

What did the inquest into Robyn Twitchell's death conclude?

An inquest was held by Judge Shubow in the Massachusetts West Roxbury District Court into the death of Robyn Twitchell to determine its cause and who was responsible for it. In his effort to understand the context of the case and of the religion and of the previous case of Dorothy Sheridan, the judge read the book by Leo Damore that I was using in my course on Law and Ethics.

At the conclusion of the inquest, the judge issued his report. In it he said that "The court fully understands it has neither the jurisdiction nor the competence to appraise the efficacy of spiritual healing as practiced by adherents of Christian Science compared with that claimed for medical science. The court has instructed itself to take care that nothing it says or concludes shall be allowed to impact adversely upon the free exercise of any person's religion, except to the extent required by law."

The judge's conclusion was that the affirmative acts and failures to act of the parents, the Christian Science nurse and the practitioner (who prayed with and for the child), and the official spokesperson for the Christian Science Church (he was a lawyer) with whom the parents had consulted all "individually and collectively contributed to the death of Robyn Twitchell. The primary cause of death was, however, from so-called natural causes" which the judge said "could readily have been prevented." Further, he noted that the question of whether the acts and omissions were unlawful must concern "the obligation of the Commonwealth to protect the right to life of a child at a time when he is totally dependent and not yet competent to make his own religious choices." He also noted that, despite their religious practices, the Twitchells had had dental care and eyeglasses care for themselves. While at that time Massachusetts law said that parents could not be considered neglectful because they relied on spiritual care, the question in the case was whether they could be considered culpable of manslaughter if their child died as a result of that care.

The Judge concluded his inquest by saying, "The inquiry has proceeded on the premise that 'parental rights do not clothe the parent with life and death authority over children.' The same premise has guided the consideration of the role of those summonsed by the parents for aid. Certainly no system of belief, religious or otherwise, can in our law enlarge parental rights to confer such authority." He found that a number of persons contributed to the death, "without malice, but recklessly and without legal excuse."

David and Ginger Twitchell were indicted by a grand jury and convicted of involuntary manslaughter in the death of their two year old son. The three church officials were not indicted. The Twitchells were sentenced to ten years' probation with a condition of their probation being that they were required to take their three other sons to a medical doctor in instances of serious illness and for regular checkups as advocated by the American Medical Association.

What were opposing comments on the outcome of the case?

Commenting on the outcome of the trial and the sentencing, the prosecutor said that the intent of his recommendation was to protect the Twitchell's other children. A defense lawyer said that the parents "have already suffered the ultimate punishment: their son has been taken from them." The father said "I'm having trouble knowing who is going to figure out when the problem is serious and when it's a cold." The Church spokesperson said "The judge in effect tried to take the heart out of Christian Science" because spiritual healing and medical treatment could not be mixed. The prosecutor countered by claiming that the outcome fostered a "marriage" of the two. Some commentators suggested that the real beneficiary of the Twitchell trial was organized medicine. One juror, a holdout until near the end, said that the judge's charge to the jury did not allow the Twitchell's religion to play a part in the jury's decision making, that the parents were getting bad advice from Church members, and that they tried to do the best they could, never thinking that there was a possibility that their son would die. Defense lawyers filed appeals, and the Twitchells moved to New York State.

The Massachusetts Supreme Judicial Court subsequently reversed their conviction because evidence of their reliance on the official church publication and the church spokesman had not been allowed introduction into the trial. The District Attorney did not, as the Supreme Judicial Court said they could, seek a new trial if the District Attorney concluded that "such a prosecution is necessary in the interests of justice."

In the Twitchell case, all felt that they were making the moral and the legal decision. The Christian Science Church officials felt they were making the moral and legal decision in following their religion. The parents felt they were making the moral decision by observing their religion and heeding the religious and legal advice of the authorities of the Church. The inquest judge made his legal choice by expressing his legal and moral view that the behavior of the Church officials and of the Twitchells was illegal. The state felt it was making the legal and moral choice by indicting the parents and not the others. The prosecuting and defense attorneys felt the same for vigorously arguing their legal and moral view and attacking opposing legal and moral views. The trial jurors felt they were upholding their legal and moral duty by convicting the Twitchells; the trial judge by sentencing them and imposing restrictions on them; and the members of the Supreme Judicial Court by reversing and remanding the case because some evidence about the parents' reliance on Church advice had not been allowed to be introduced into the trial; and finally the District Attorney by not retrying the case. It was obvious that many of the views directly conflicted with other views, yet all of those involved seemed to feel that they had made the moral and legal decision.

Could that be possible? Where the law was concerned, divergent views became majority and dissenting opinions. While each side in a dispute considered its approach to be the legal one, the side with the greater number of adherents or the one in whose favor a decision was rendered was the legal one. What, one might ask, was the equivalent of this paradigm with regard to morality?

What was the child-abuse scandal that afflicted the Roman Catholic Church?

Whereas the practice of spiritual healing was at the foundation of the Christian Science religion; and the Massachusetts law, as interpreted by the spokesperson for and the manual of the Church, appeared to give the parents the right to follow their religion's teaching when their son became sick; neither the teaching of the Roman Catholic religion nor the Massachusetts (or others states) law gave priests even the appearance of permission to sexually molest children in their care, or their superiors to cover it up and to transfer priests from one parish to another giving them continual opportunities to molest children with only somewhat brief breaks for treatment and with no notice to the receiving parishes.

That lack of care of children became the scandal of the Roman Catholic Church which cost it great sums of money and considerable public scorn. While the Church eventually apologized to some extent, it also rewarded a Cardinal in Boston at the heart of the scandal by granting him supervision over one of the four most prestigious churches in Rome. It appeared that his consistent vocal support for the Church position on abortion and homosexuality outweighed the practice he knew about and countenanced and covered up of (largely) homosexual predatory behavior by priests for whom he was responsible.

What were the legal and moral dimensions of the Roman Catholic Church scandal?

The Boston Globe broke the story of what it termed "the crisis in the Catholic Church" in articles in its newspaper by its Investigative Team and then in narrative form in its book called *Betrayal*, the Introduction to which set out the dimensions of the scandal. "*Betrayal* is the story of a large number of Catholic priests who abused both the trust given them and the children in their care. It is the story of the bishops and the cardinals who hired, promoted, protected, and thanked those priests, despite overwhelming evidence of their abusive behavior." "It is the story of victims who suffered in silence for years." Further, the Team said that "reports showed that members of the Church hierarchy—including Cardinal Bernard F. Law of Boston, the most influential American Catholic prelate with the Vatican—were not only aware of the abuse" "but had engaged in such a massive cover-up." "The extent of betrayal—of children's innocence, of parents' trust, of priestly vows, of bishops' responsibilities, of the Church's basic tenets—was unnerving." And then in almost three hundred pages, the book detailed the enormous gap between the Church teachings and the Church practices. For those who read the book, it was an appalling recital of lack of care and concern for children, of rampant hypocrisy, of righteous preaching and unlawful practice, and of immoral men holding themselves out as moral exemplars.

And while some priests went to jail subsequently for their predatory sexual behavior, the statutes of limitations prevented charging most with crimes. Eventually, after trying to prevent civil suits, the Church was forced to settle with victims who brought suits. In September 2007, for example, the San Diego Catholic Diocese reached a settlement of $198 million with abuse victims, while earlier a judge approved the largest settlement until then of $660 million between the Archdiocese of Los Angeles and 508 victims. And those did not include settlements in Boston and in many other locations.

Not only did the cover-up involve those in the hierarchy of the church, it involved those whose task it was to evaluate and treat the priests who were abusing. According to press reports at the time, the priest/psychiatrist who had headed the Treaters Group at the Massachusetts General Hospital was reputed to have known most about the abusers and the victims. As a Jesuit priest, he was not a mandated reporter under the Massachusetts law before 2002, but as a Massachusetts General Hospital psychiatrist he was. Nonetheless, press reports indicated that he never contacted authorities about any abusive priest, despite dealing with many. When asked if he ever advised the archdiocese "to contact law enforcement or child protection agencies" he was reported to have replied "I don't remember that I did."

As one legal consequence of the publicity about the abuse, states reconsidered their statutes of limitations on the reporting of crimes, and included priests and others among the mandated reporters of child abuse, sexual and otherwise.

As a moral consequence of the scandal, questions were raised about the culture of the priesthood, the issue of celibacy, the Church's teachings on homosexuality, the moral hypocrisy of the Church, and the extent of the systemic problems within it.

Concerning priests' predatory behavior and the hierarchy's cover-up, how did the Roman Catholic Church balance verbal adherence to its moral precepts with practical implementation and oversight of some of them?

One consequence of Boston's Cardinal Law's inability to keep quiet the behavior of priests and of him and others in the Church hierarchy was that he resigned as archbishop of Boston. But the Church rewarded him for his stated adherence to its moral precepts, especially with regard to its adamant stand against abortion. He maintained the Church position that abortion was immoral and should be illegal in all instances. After his resignation, *Boston Magazine* reported that he "remains a highly respected member of the Catholic Church's hierarchy in Rome," where he was appointed to run one of the four patriarchal basilicas and lived in splendor, despite the disgrace in which he was held in Boston and the crisis he and others precipitated in the Roman Catholic Church. His closeness to then Pope John Paul II and his adherence to the Catholic doctrine had evidently outweighed his lack of care for children, his hypocrisy, and his moral failings.

5

Capital Punishment

What is the nature of the moral and legal problem?

An issue argued vigorously by proponents of two different ethical and legal views is clearly a moral problem of importance. The legal statutes and decisions, and the immense amount of commentary about the death penalty, though it is rarely used, make it an important topic for this book. Whether the state should put someone found guilty of a heinous crime to death contains all the elements which necessitate legal and moral decision making.

What are arguments against the death penalty?

Those who consider the death penalty immoral and oppose it do so for a number of reasons. Among them are the following. If a mistake should be made, the penalty is irreversible. The state's taking a life sets a bad example and actually fosters the taking of lives. Revenge is unworthy of a civilized society. The nature of the punishment is itself cruel and unusual. Empirical evidence about whether it deters crimes is inconclusive. The punishment brutalizes all those who administer it. The codes of ethics of the medical profession prevent physicians from participating in executions. Society itself becomes a murderer by executing individuals. And, as many have argued, it is governed by caprice and mistake.

What arguments favor the death penalty?

Those who consider the death penalty moral and favor it also do so for a number of reasons. Among them are the following. It should be reserved for the most serious offenses and when the evidence is absolutely clear so mistakes will not be made. The state's taking a life sets a good example and shows the limit of what the state will tolerate in terms of antisocial, unconscionable behavior. Retribution, or just desserts, is moral because it sets the boundaries of the intolerable and accords to each individual the dignity of responding sufficiently to his or her acts. The nature of the punishment is not unusual, though quite limited, and not cruel, if administered humanely. Capital punishment may be the only deterrent for some persons, as of an inmate serving the maximum of a life sentence who can then kill a prison official without fear of further punishment. The punishment brutalizes no more than does war or self-defense killing. And society is not a murderer by executing convicted criminals because murder is unlawful killing and executions are lawful killing following due process accorded to individuals.

What is the moral problem with the nature of punishment itself?

Beyond the fact of capital punishment there is the moral problem of the nature of the punishment itself. And at least three theories of punishment are advanced. One is the utilitarian theory of punishment. According to it, the purpose of punishment is to promote the general good by deterring others from committing injustices. This theory looks to the future, attempts to discover what the future result of a certain course of action will be, how best to maximize future happiness of the greatest number through the imposition of sanctions at the present time. Under the utilitarian theory, the punishment of an innocent person as an example could be justified if that produced the greatest happiness of the greatest number of individuals, regardless of what one might say is the injustice to the one individual punished for an act he did not commit. The utilitarian view looks to the group, not the individual; to the future end, not to the past; to the calculation of greatest benefit to the greatest number. The objections to the utilitarian theory of punishment center on its potential for injustice to the individual and on its emphasis on the future rather than the past.

A second theory of punishment is the retributivist theory. According to this theory, the purpose of punishment is to provide just desserts for the individual who commits an injustice. This theory looks to the past and attempts to discover what the fit or just result of a past course of action ought to be, how best to make the individual who has committed a wrong act suffer at the present time, to correct the moral balance. Under the retributivist notion, the punishment of an innocent person could not be justified for that person would merit no punishment. The retributivist view looks to the individual, not the group; to the past, not to the future; to the calculation of just desserts for the individual, not the greatest happiness for the greatest number. The major objections to the retributivist theory of punishment center on what is termed its focus on revenge.

A third theory is related to these two theories of punishment. But that third theory rejects punishment in favor of rehabilitation. According to that theory, the purpose of treatment, not punishment, is to restore the individual who has committed an injustice to a just, moral way of thinking and acting. The objections to the rehabilitative theory center on the large amount of research which suggests that rehabilitation does not work; and on the notion that acts ought to have consequences, and that bad acts ought to have bad consequences for those who commit them.

Beyond these theories there is a further question: is there a right to punishment? Do individuals have a moral right to be punished for their wrong acts? It has been argued that this right to punishment acknowledges the personhood of individuals, confers on them the dignity of suggesting they are responsible individuals, and suggests that they have a moral right to reward as well. By extension, it has been further argued that all individuals, including the young, the mentally ill, and others often thought excused from punishment, equally have a right to the dignity and respect that the right to punishment confers. But as subsequent questions address, that right does not extend to capital punishment as the Supreme Court has found the death penalty unconstitutional if applied to juveniles or to the mentally retarded. The Court has not yet followed up those decisions with a consideration of the mentally ill.

What was the progression of U.S. Supreme Court cases concerning capital punishment?

Since 1976, four significant cases concerned capital punishment. In the first of these, Furman v. Georgia, the Supreme Court decided that capital punishment as then practiced by the states was unconstitutional under the U.S. Constitution. In the second of these, Gregg v. Georgia, the Supreme Court decided that the revisions that states made to their death penalty statutes rendered them constitutional. In the third of these, Atkins v. Virginia, the Supreme Court ruled that it was unconstitutional to execute the mentally retarded. And in the fourth of these, Roper v. Simmons, the Court decided that it was unconstitutional to execute juveniles.

What were the reasons that Furman v. Georgia ruled capital punishment unconstitutional?

In 1972, the U.S. Supreme Court ruled that the death penalty, as then administered, was unconstitutional. It found that the penalty was imposed in an arbitrary or capricious manner because inadequate information about the nature and circumstances of the offense, and about the character and record of the offender were given to the sentencing authority, nor was there sufficient guidance as to how to make the decision about death or life.

In ruling on the death penalty, the Court addressed the argument that the death penalty was always, whatever the heinousness of the offense and whatever the procedure followed in determining the sentence, cruel and unusual punishment in violation of the U. S. Constitution. As the Supreme Court said in its later opinion in Gregg v. Georgia, "Four Justices would have held that capital punishment is not unconstitutional per se; two Justices would have reached the opposite conclusion; and three Justices, while agreeing that the statutes then before the Court were invalid as applied, left open the question whether such punishment may ever be imposed."

What were the reasons that Gregg v. Georgia ruled capital punishment constitutional?

In 1976, Justice Stewart, writing for the majority in the case of Gregg v. Georgia, said that "The issue in this case is whether the imposition of the sentence of death for the crime of murder under the law of Georgia violates the Eighth and Fourteenth Amendments" to the U.S. Constitution. After a trial in two stages, first guilt then sentencing, Gregg was convicted of armed robbery and murder and sentenced to death. The procedures the Legislature had enacted since the Furman case rectified the defects noted in that earlier opinion. The Supreme Court now ruled that the punishment of death did not violate the Constitution, effectively reinstating the death penalty in the United States.

In interpreting the Eighth Amendment, the Court wrote that "the Eighth Amendment has not been regarded as a static concept. As Chief Justice Warren said, in an oft-quoted phrase, 'the Amendment must draw its meaning from the evolving standards of decency that mark the progress of a maturing society.' Thus, an assessment of contemporary values concerning the infliction of a challenged sanction is relevant to the application of the Eighth Amendment." So the court looked both to objective evidence of the public's attitude toward the death penalty and to the matter of the "dignity of man" to determine whether the punishment of death is "excessive." It must not involve "the unnecessary and wanton infliction of pain" or "be grossly out of proportion to the severity of the crime."

At the same time, the Supreme Court was mindful of its role which was different from that of legislators. The Court reflected that "in assessing a punishment selected by a democratically elected legislature against the constitutional measure, we presume its validity. We may not require the legislature to select the least severe penalty possible so long as the penalty selected is not cruelly inhumane or disproportionate to the crime involved. And a heavy burden rests on those who would attack the judgment of the representatives of the people."

And the Court quoted from the earlier case of Furman v. Georgia: "In a democratic society, legislatures, not courts, are constituted to respond to the will and consequently the moral values of the people." And following the originalist view of interpretation, the Court noted that the death penalty was accepted at the time of the founding of the United States.

Further the Court looked to the fact that, since Furman, society had endorsed the death penalty for murder: "The legislatures of at least 35 States have enacted new statutes that provide for the death penalty for at least some crimes that result in the death of another person. And the Congress of the United States, in 1974, enacted a statute providing the death penalty for aircraft piracy that results in death." Further it asserted that "The jury also is a significant and reliable objective index of contemporary values because it is so directly involved."

The Court went on: "Considerations of federalism, as well as respect for the ability of a legislature to evaluate, in terms of its particular State, the moral consensus concerning the death penalty and its social utility as a sanction, require us to conclude, in the absence of more convincing evidence, that the infliction of death as a punishment for murder is not without justification and thus is not unconstitutionally severe."

What was the basis of a dissenting opinion in the Gregg v. Georgia case?

Justice Brennan dissented on what he termed "moral grounds." He wrote that "This Court inescapably has the duty, as the ultimate arbiter of the meaning of our Constitution, to say whether, when individuals condemned to death stand before our Bar, 'moral concepts' require us to hold that the law has progressed to the point where we should declare that the punishment of death, like punishments on the rack, the screw, and the wheel, is no longer morally tolerable in our civilized society." He concluded that the death penalty was no longer morally tolerable in the United States despite the evidence the majority used to declare that it was morally tolerable.

What was the basis of another dissenting opinion in that case?

In Furman, Justice Marshall had concluded that the death penalty was cruel and unusual punishment prohibited by the Eighth and Fourteenth Amendments because it was excessive and because the American people lacked sufficient information about it. In Gregg, he wrote that in Furman he concluded that "the American people, fully informed as to the purposes of the death penalty and its liabilities, would in my view reject it as morally unacceptable." But he acknowledged in the later case that "Since the decision in Furman, the legislatures of 35 States have enacted new statutes authorizing the imposition of the death sentence for certain crimes, and Congress has enacted a law providing the death penalty for air piracy resulting in death. I would be less than candid if I did not acknowledge that these developments have a significant bearing on a realistic assessment of the moral acceptability of the death penalty to the American people. But if the constitutionality of the death penalty turns, as I have urged, on the opinion of an informed citizenry, then even the enactment of new death statutes cannot be viewed as conclusive. In Furman, I observed that the American people are largely unaware of the information critical to a judgment on the morality of the death penalty, and concluded that if they were better informed they would consider it shocking, unjust and unacceptable."

In one sense Justice Marshall could not, in his own mind, be wrong. If the legislatures had reflected his view by rejecting the death penalty, then he would conclude that they were better informed; if, on the other hand, the legislatures did not, as they did not, reflect his view then he could believe that they were still not sufficiently "an informed citizenry" and that, whatever they thought, his view remained that the death penalty was excessive and therefore unconstitutional. He did not believe that taking a murderer's life was "itself morally good."

What were the reasons that Atkins v. Virginia ruled the capital punishment of mentally retarded persons unconstitutional?

In 2002, the Supreme Court ruled that executing mentally retarded persons was "cruel and unusual punishment" in violation of the Eighth Amendment to the U.S. Constitution. Justice Stevens noted that a significant number of states had already concluded that the death penalty was not suitable for such persons. The Court applied the "evolving standards of decency" test and found that the punishment of death was excessive especially as both retribution and deterrence were less effective or ineffective with mentally retarded individuals. What dissenters questioned was the unclear standard, the difficulty of determining the factors which constituted mental retardation, and the opportunity such a ruling brought for turning a capital trial "into a game," as Justice Scalia argued. In Atkins' trial, for example, one defense forensic psychologist testified that Atkins was mildly retarded, and then at a second sentencing hearing repeated his conclusion, but a State expert contradicted that conclusion about Atkins' intelligence.

What were the reasons that Roper v. Simmons ruled the capital punishment of minors unconstitutional?

In 2004, the Supreme Court ruled in a 5-4 opinion that executing minors violated the prohibition in the Eighth Amendment to the U.S. Constitution on "cruel and unusual punishment" (which the Court noted was applied to the states through the Fourteenth Amendment). Again, the Court relied on the test of "evolving standards of decency" and noted that many state legislatures had changed their laws to remove juveniles from those subject to execution. The majority also looked to other countries' prohibitions on executing minors as evidence of an international consensus against the practice, and contended that the Court should take this international consensus into account.

What might be the next group whose execution would be considered an example of "cruel and unusual punishment"?

Although the composition of the U.S. Supreme Court had changed since the capital punishment prohibitions for the mentally retarded and minors, advocates against the death penalty in general, but who were proceeding a group at a time for practical reasons, indicated that the mentally ill might be the next test for the U.S. Supreme Court. Short of an outright prohibition on capital punishment as "cruel and unusual," those advocates considered the successes they already achieved as preludes to more successes to come.

On what basis did the Massachusetts Supreme Judicial Court conclude that capital punishment violated its own state constitution?

In 1980, the Massachusetts Supreme Judicial Court ruled that capital punishment violated its own Constitution's prohibition on cruel and unusual punishment. In his concurring opinion in the case of District Attorney v. Watson, Massachusetts Supreme Court Justice Liacos wrote: "Death is the 'king of terrors.' Job 18:14. Aristotle called death 'the most terrible of all things; for it is the end, and nothing is thought to be any longer either good or bad for the dead.' So deep is the fear of death and the corresponding desire for transcendence that Christian thought attributes death to the fall of Adam, and the New Testament proclaims Christ's victory over death. I Corinthians 15:20, 26. Psychiatrists have observed that terror of death is at the root of much mental disease."

And he also noted: "A condemned man knows, subject to the possibility of successful appeal or commutation, the time and manner of his death. Apart from cases of suicide or terminal illness, this certainty is unique to those who are sentenced to death. The State puts the question of death to the condemned person, and he must grapple with it without the consolation that he will die naturally or with his humanity intact. A condemned person experiences an extreme form of debasement."

In a dissenting opinion, Justice Quirico wrote that the Court "must, at a minimum, award great deference to the legislative judgment implicit in the passage of the statute that contemporary moral standards support the punishment in certain circumstances. There is no apparent reason why the nearly identical State and Federal constitutional provisions should not dictate identical results."

He recalled "that 'legislatures are ultimate guardians of the liberties and welfare of the people in quite as great a degree as the courts.'" And he wrote: "A vote on the subject of capital punishment by a member of the general public or by a member of the Legislature requires a consideration of broad questions of public policy. A vote on the same subject as it comes before the court in this case involves consideration of the much more limited constitutional questions of the power of the Legislature to determine what the public policy of the Commonwealth should be on this subject. I conclude that the Legislature has the power to make that decision under the provisions of the Constitution of this Commonwealth, and I reach that conclusion without regard to any personal views which I may have on the 'expediency, wisdom or necessity' of capital punishment."

As with the Justices on the U.S. Supreme Court, the Justices of the Massachusetts Supreme Judicial Court relied on two different approaches to whose view should prevail in matters of moral decision making, the legislature representing the will of the majority through its elected representatives or the judiciary reflecting the enlightened, evolving standard of decency in a maturing society.

What did public opinion polls show about its view of capital punishment?

Justice Marshall wrote in Furman and referred to it in Gregg that an informed public would react against the death penalty. One approach to resolving a legal and ethical dilemma is to examine public opinion. Those public opinion polls found popular support for capital punishment in the United States. An ABC News/Washington Post poll reported in mid-2006 that 65% of adults favored the death penalty for persons convicted of murder, while 32% opposed it and 3% were unsure. A Gallup Poll reported about the same time that 21% of adults thought the death penalty was imposed too often, 25% thought it was imposed about the right amount, and 51% thought it was imposed not often enough, totaling 76% support. According to those and many other polls, a large number of adults favored death as a legal and moral response to a heinous crime. Legal and moral decision making in the United States differed from Western Europe and approximately 60 other nations where capital punishment was abolished.

Further, when asked in mid-2005 in a Fox News/Opinion Dynamics Poll whether they favored the death penalty for juveniles, 26% did and 69% opposed it; for the mentally retarded, 13% favored it and 82% opposed it; for the mentally ill, 19% favored it and 75% opposed it.

And when asked in an ABC News/Washington Post poll in mid-2005 who they trusted more to deal with the issue of the death penalty, 40% replied their state legislature, 53% their state courts, 1% both equally, 4% neither, and 1% were unsure.

Is one method of execution more legal or more moral than others?

Various methods were and are available to carry out a sentence of death: electric chair, gallows, gas chamber, lethal injection, and firing squad among them. Some states gave the offender a choice. In most instances, the means of execution were in good working order. But sometimes the means faltered. In Florida, smoke and flames leaped from the electrodes on one prisoner's head. According to accounts, it took three surges of electricity and a few more minutes to kill the convicted killer. In Georgia, a second charge of electricity was required after a murderer struggled to breathe for eight minutes following the first charge. In Texas, an execution was delayed for fourteen minutes when a tube from an intravenous needle began to leak. Opponents of the death penalty pointed to these examples to argue that the penalty was itself immoral and its botched administration further evidence that it was practically, as well as theoretically, wrong. Even when the administration of the death penalty was not botched, questions arose about its morality and legality. The U.S. Supreme Court agreed to review a capital punishment case from Kentucky, Baze v. Rees. As Linda Greenhouse reported in *The New York Times*, "The issue in that case is not the constitutionality of lethal injection as such, but rather a more procedural question: how judges should evaluate claims that the particular combination of drugs used to bring about death causes suffering that amounts to cruel and unusual punishment, in violation of the Eighth Amendment."

Is life imprisonment a suitable legal or moral alternative to capital punishment?

States have been reluctant to impose a sentence of life in prison without any possibility of parole or release. Killers were almost always considered for parole or eligible for commutation of a sentence. And some killers killed while in prison. A case such as that of Samuel Smith put this issue in perspective.

Samuel Smith, while in his early 40s had committed crimes for a quarter century. He confessed to five murders, to rapes, kidnappings, assaults and robberies. He was in prison in New York with a maximum sentence of 25 years to life. He had a chance for parole so he had something left to lose if he killed while in prison. Nonetheless, he murdered a prison guard, strangling her and stuffing her mutilated body in the prison trash. Proponents of the death penalty argued that no-hope lifers, at the least, needed the sanction of the death penalty. Opponents of the death penalty advocated stricter isolation of such prisoners within the institution. Yet, when Smith was given an administrative sentence of 15 years in housing set apart from the prison premises, his lawyer called the sentence solitary confinement and termed it obviously illegal. To protect society, some commentators urged separating such killers permanently from society, not by execution, but by exiling them to some distant islands. Of course, unless each had his own island, there would be the chance that some violent criminal might kill another on the island. The innocent, at least, it was said, would be spared.

The death penalty was infrequently implemented throughout the United States, more in some jurisdictions, none in others. The choice between life imprisonment as it was implemented and the death penalty caused many to argue for the acceleration of capital punishment. Yet, when questioned in an ABC News/Washington Post Poll in mid-2006, 50% of adults preferred the death penalty for people convicted of murder while 46% preferred life in prison with no chance of parole and 5% were unsure.

Additional questions abounded in the controversy between advocates of capital punishment and advocates of life imprisonment: Could offenders be rehabilitated? Was death too severe a penalty however heinous, brutal or repeated the violent act? Should age or mental status simply be a factor to be considered rather than an absolute bar to capital punishment?

6

Right to Die

What kind of problem is the right to die?

The right to die is a moral, philosophical, social, legal, political, religious, and medical problem. Among the questions raised are the following. What is life for? Should the quality of one's life count in moral decision making? What is the difference between extending life and prolonging death? What constitutes death? Who decides these issues? Is there a right to death with dignity? Is there a right of privacy where death is concerned? Can suicide be rational? To what extent, if any, might doctors help individuals end their lives? Is euthanasia moral? Ought it be legal? What does terminal mean in relation to the amount of time remaining? Do the elderly and very ill have a duty to die? What positions do various religions have on this problem?

Whereas capital punishment involves the state's taking the life of an offender, the right to die involves the decision of an individual to end his or her own life or the decision of others to end that life. But both capital punishment and right to die involve life and death issues. Applying issues raised by the death penalty to the right to die suggests still more questions. Among them are these. Can one be condemned to life? If the guilty are assisted in their deaths through execution, ought the innocent who want help in dying to receive it using similar methods if they wish? If botched executions of the guilty horrify and are to be avoided, why do not botched deaths of the innocent (through ineffective attempts at suicide or through the drawn-out degrading process of natural death) horrify as well and suggest they are to be avoided? Are such deaths and lives cruel and unusual punishment whether implemented by men and women or by nature? How explicit must living wills or medical directives or health care powers of attorney be to insure their maker's wish will be carried out?

What did the U.S. Supreme Court decide in the Cruzan v. Director, Missouri Department of Health case?

This 1990 case, the first in which the U.S. Supreme Court decided a right to die case, concerned a woman left in a persistent vegetative state as a result of an automobile accident. Her parents, who were her co-guardians, sought a lower court order to discontinue her artificial feeding and hydration because she had no chance of recovering her cognitive functioning. The Supreme Court of Missouri held that there was no "clear and convincing evidence" of her desire to have the treatment withdrawn and as a result the parents' request could not be accommodated. The U.S. Supreme Court affirmed that decision.

Chief Justice Rehnquist wrote for the majority that such an important act necessitated "heightened evidentiary requirements" which, because Cruzan had no written document of any kind, could not be met.

What did a concurring opinion conclude about the role of the judiciary in such life and death matters?

A concurring opinion by Justice Scalia clearly stated his views about the role of the court in determining such life and death matters. He wrote "that the federal courts have no business in this field; that American law has always accorded the State the power to prevent, by force if necessary, suicide including suicide by refusing to take appropriate measures necessary to preserve one's life; that the point at which life becomes 'worthless,' and the point at which the means necessary to preserve it become 'extraordinary' or 'inappropriate,' are neither set forth in the Constitution nor known to the nine Justices of this Court any better than they are known to nine people picked at random from the Kansas City telephone directory; and hence, that even when it is demonstrated by clear and convincing evidence that a patient no longer wishes certain measures to be taken to preserve her life, it is up to the citizens of Missouri to decide, through their elected representatives, whether that wish will be honored. It is quite possible (because the Constitution says nothing about the matter) that those citizens will decide upon a line less lawful than the one we would choose; and it is unlikely (because we know no more about 'life and death' than they do) that they will decide upon a line less reasonable.

"Our salvation is the Equal Protection Clause, which requires the democratic majority to accept for themselves and their loved ones what they impose on you and me. This Court need not, and has no authority to, inject itself into every field of human activity where irrationality and oppression may theoretically occur, and if it tries to do so it will destroy itself."

What did a dissenting opinion conclude about the requirements for making one's wishes known?

Justice Brennan wrote in his dissent about the requirements for making one's wishes known. He noted that "Too few people execute living wills or equivalently formal directives for such an evidentiary rule to ensure adequately that the wishes of incompetent persons will be honored. While it might be wise social policy to encourage people to furnish such instructions, no general conclusion about a patient's choice can be drawn from the absence of formalities."

He further wrote: "The Missouri court's disdain for Nancy's statements in serious conversations not long before her accident, for the opinions of Nancy's family and friends as to her values, beliefs and certain choice, and even for the opinion of an outside objective fact finder appointed by the State evinces a disdain for Nancy Cruzan's own right to choose." "Missouri and this Court have displaced Nancy's own assessment of the processes associated with dying. They have discarded evidence of her will, ignored her values, and deprived her of the right to a decision as closely approximating her own choice as humanly possible."

What did a dissenting opinion conclude about the effort to define the meaning of life?

Justice Stevens wrote in his dissent: "Our ethical tradition has long regarded an appreciation of mortality as essential to understanding life's significance. These considerations cast into stark relief the injustice, and unconstitutionality, of Missouri's treatment of Nancy Beth Cruzan. For patients like Nancy Cruzan, who have no consciousness and no chance of recovery, there is a serious question as to whether the mere persistence of their bodies is 'life' as that word is commonly understood, or as it is used in both the Constitution and the Declaration of Independence. The State's unflagging determination to perpetuate Nancy Cruzan's physical existence is comprehensible only as an effort to define life's meaning, not as an attempt to preserve its sanctity."

What are moral obligations to dying family members?

In an early book, *Last Wish*, on the moral obligation to help a dying family member, Betty Rollin told of helping her mother die. Her mother-in-law had died slowly of cancer, becoming shriveled, in constant pain, brittle boned, constipated, in and out of a morphine haze. She had emphatically wanted to die. Betty Rollin's mother, who had untreatable ovarian cancer, did not want to die that way. She asked her daughter to get her the drugs with which to commit suicide. Her daughter complied with her mother's wish. The book detailed the explicit method she used. An overseas doctor who secured the medicine for her also advised Ms. Rollin how to cause the death, and cautioned her and her husband to be careful because of the legal jeopardy in which they might find themselves for providing the information and materials to her mother. The doctor said to Ms. Rollin: "People should have the right to end their lives when they want to, and if they need help to do it, so be it." Her mother died as a result of her daughter's providing for her last wish, and even with the publication of the book Ms. Rollin was not charged in her mother's death.

What are the objections to helping a family member die?

Many physicians and ethicists and disabled have written or spoken about their abhorrence of such acts. They have focused on adequate pain medication to alleviate suffering, on the provision of hospice care, and similar measures. Advocates for the disabled, including the group Not Dead Yet, have demonstrated against assisted suicide and euthanasia. All those who are opposed to family members or professionals assisting with death view the process as devaluing life, as a slippery slope toward explicit or implicit urgings that the terminally ill or the disabled have a duty to die.

What was the view of the author of Prescription Medicide?

In 1993, Dr. Jack Kevorkian wrote a book about The goodness of planned death which he called *Prescription Medicide*. Though a part of it dealt with his then well-known suicide machine, about two-thirds of the book dealt with his argument for harvesting for transplantation the organs of those condemned to death. Neither argument had much political, legislative, judicial, or moral support. Though he had participated in what was termed self-deliverance by those using his machine, he had never been convicted. He decided he needed to take his position to a wider audience and to challenge the authorities to legalize physician-assisted suicide and euthanasia or to charge him.

Why did Washington v. Glucksberg rule that a state ban on physician-assisted suicide was constitutional?

Before Jack Kevorkian could engage the wider audience he was seeking, the U.S. Supreme Court ruled in 1997 against physician-assisted suicide. The Court held that the State of Washington's ban on physician-assisted suicide, denying competent terminally ill adults the freedom to choose death over life, did not violate the Fourteenth Amendment's Due Process Clause. Further, the unanimous decision of the Court argued that the right to assisted suicide was not a fundamental liberty interest because it was and is offensive to national traditions and practices. And the Court reasoned that the Washington state prohibition protected medical ethics; protected disabled and terminally ill individuals who might be coerced, directly or indirectly, into ending their lives; and preserved human life.

Did the case of Vacco v. Quill conclude there was a difference between active and passive withdrawing of lifesaving treatment?

Also in 1997, the U.S. Supreme Court ruled against physician-assisted suicide. It held that New York State's ban did not violate the Fourteenth Amendment's Equal Protection Clause. The Court did not consider the seeming contradiction between allowing terminally ill adults who were competent to withdraw their own lifesaving treatment, while not allowing patients who were too disabled to withdraw their own lifesaving treatment from having a physician do it for them. Again, the Court reasoned that the state protected medical ethics; prevented euthanasia; protected the disabled and terminally ill individuals who might be coerced, directly or indirectly, into ending their lives; and preserved human life. The Court also differentiated the two instances by focusing on the criminal intent in causing the death of another person.

How did an advocate of the right to die escalate his behavior in an effort to force the law to change to permit both physician-assisted suicide and euthanasia?

Having assisted in numerous suicides by those who sought him out, Dr. Jack Kevorkian was never convicted of a crime. He argued that his behavior was moral. Prosecutors and others argued that his behavior was both immoral and illegal. Because of all this, Kevorkian decided to escalate his behavior in an effort to force the law to change to permit both physician-assisted suicide and euthanasia.

Because he had not been able to make his point with past efforts, Kevorkian decided in 1998 to videotape his administering a lethal injection to a man who had requested his assistance. Thomas Youk, in the later stages of what was called Lou Gehrig's disease, requested Kevorkian's assistance in dying. Kevorkian complied, in defiance of the law, by administering a lethal injection of potassium chloride. He videotaped his interviewing Youk and administering the injection. But, when nothing happened as a result of his action, Kevorkian decided to make his video public. He gave the video to the television program *60 Minutes* and the program televised that video. Accompanying the Kevorkian videotape were interviews with Youk's family who supported what happened; as well as Kevorkian's reflecting on this case and on the issues raised by physician-assisted suicide and by euthanasia.

On the program, Kevorkian told the interviewer Mike Wallace that he had moved from physician-assisted suicide, where he had helped over 100 people end their lives, to active mercy killing in order to advance the debate concerning euthanasia. He had provided the videotape to *60 Minutes* in order to force the state to confront directly the issue. Youk's family, interviewed for the program, approved of his and Kevorkian's decisions and actions. Three days later the state of Michigan charged Kevorkian with first-degree murder. Though *60 Minutes* said at the time that it was advancing the public's knowledge concerning the issues of physician-assisted suicide and mercy killing, it later had second thoughts about whether it was appropriate to show such a program, especially during the so-called family viewing time.

What ethical questions were raised by the 60 Minutes *broadcast?*

The program raised a number of ethical questions. Among them were the following. Should *60 Minutes* have aired the videotape? Should Youk have requested physician-assisted suicide? Should Youk's family have attempted to persuade him against the course of action or intervened to prevent it if they were not successful in their effort? Should Kevorkian have performed the action? Should the state have prosecuted Kevorkian? Should a jury have nullified the law and found Kevorkian not guilty? Should Kevorkian have been sentenced to prison?

What were ethical objections to airing the physician-assisted suicide on 60 Minutes?

Many ethicists disagreed with *60 Minutes'* decision to air the program. One line of their argument concluded that the program sensationalized the issues, was in poor taste, and was offensive to many in the audience as it made death a public spectacle. They argued that harm to a great many and to the sanctity of life flowed from the airing. They said that the program contributed to a culture of death, to a desensitization toward end of life issues, and to potential harm to the disabled, who may be expected to die as Youk had done. They said it was unrealistic to say that individuals should simply turn off their television sets. Rather, the program, the government, or some similar group or organization ought to protect vulnerable individuals from seeing such material by not showing it. Further, they said that the showing invaded Youk's privacy, and even though he appeared to permit that invasion and realized that the tape would be aired, he was in no condition to make a freely-determined choice in the matter. They said that better end of life care, by physicians, in hospices was a necessary improvement in the care of the dying and that those measures would replace any need for physician-assisted suicide or euthanasia.

What were arguments supporting 60 Minutes' *decision to air the death?*

Those who agreed with the showing said that the public needed to see Youk's condition, his request to Kevorkian, his family's approval of the act itself, and Kevorkian's response to criticisms. They concluded that public debate could be informed by such information and that actual viewing was preferable to the filter of summarizers, commentators, and others who were not involved with the decisions and acts. They advocated individual self-determination in end of life decisions. They argued that the program would spur persons, legislatures, courts to consider the issues of end-of-life care, including pain medication, more extensively, as well as the physician-assisted suicide and euthanasia that Kevorkian had advocated. At the time of the program, and to the present, only the State of Oregon legalized physician-assisted suicide, not euthanasia, and the federal government continued to attempt to overturn that law. Finally, many concluded that Kevorkian had advanced the debate about the issue of physician-assisted suicide, though not the issue of euthanasia.

What was a follow-up to the broadcast?

60 Minutes later broadcast a segment that showed sick people who opposed assisted suicide. Youk's relatives said they were upset with that segment in which one dying person said that Youk had "simply wimped out." Pro-life viewers were upset about the initial segment which showed Kevorkian administering the lethal injection. Some questioned the timing of the follow-up because it came a week after the original news correspondent had noted that he had second thoughts about the initial broadcast.

What was the outcome of that advocate's trial and sentencing?

The tape of Youk's death by injection became the major piece of evidence to charge Jack Kevorkian with first-degree murder, assisted suicide, and illegal use of a controlled substance. He was convicted. Youk's wife and brother asked the judge at the sentencing hearing not to jail Kevorkian. They argued that Tom Youk had wanted to end his suffering and that Kevorkian had acted to end suffering. But in 1998, Michigan voters, by more than two to one, rejected a ballot referendum question to legalize assisted suicide.

In 1999, a Michigan judge sentenced Kevorkian to ten to twenty-five years in prison for the second-degree murder of Thomas Youk. Kevorkian became eligible for parole on May 26, 2007. A spokesperson for the disability-rights group Not Dead Yet said, "We hope that he will never get out of prison." "He has shown an utter contempt for the law and a deadly contempt for us." Kevorkian, however, was paroled on the promise that he would not participate in any further physician-assisted suicide or euthanasia.

What did the decision in Gonzales v. Oregon conclude about physician prescriptions of lethal doses under Death with Dignity Act?

In 1994, Oregon enacted the Death with Dignity Act, permitting physicians to prescribe lethal doses of controlled substances to terminally ill patients, in effect assisting the patients if they chose suicide. The Gonzales v. Oregon case resulted from the State of Oregon's suit originally against then-Attorney General John Ashcroft's threat, under the 1970 Controlled Substances Act, to revoke the medical licenses of physicians who participated. The Supreme Court held that the Attorney General, Alberto Gonzales at the time of the decision, was not authorized by that federal act to declare a medical procedure authorized by a state act law illegal. The purpose of the federal Act was to prevent illicit drug dealing not to evaluate medical practice within a state. Oregon remained the only state with such a Death with Dignity Act.

Administrative Issues

7

Affirmative Action

What is the moral and legal decision about affirmative action?

Affirmative action, as is true of the topics that follow, invokes issues less dramatic than life and death, but nevertheless the social issue is significant. While termed administrative practices, they are that and more, raising important moral problems.

Affirmative action appeared specifically in the Civil Rights Act of 1964 concerning employment and in an Executive Order applying to federal contracts. Programs of affirmative action were implemented in desegregation of public schools, in housing, and in employment. In this book affirmative action in higher education will be the focus.

What legal questions are raised by affirmative action?

An essential legal question about affirmative action was whether it violated the equal protection of the laws guaranteed by the Fourteenth Amendment to the U.S. Constitution and by the colorblind language of the Civil Rights Act of 1964, or whether it was a lawful method of dealing with historic discrimination toward blacks especially, and toward others. Questions which it raised included these. Was it constitutional to decide admissions or other similarly important matters on the basis of race? If so, how was race to be determined? If it were, how was it best to go about it? What factors ought to be taken into account? What standards of decision making ought to be used? Were the decisions that were constitutional the same as decisions that were moral? Or were moral standards and constitutional standards different to a smaller or larger extent? What, if anything, distinguished them?

A further issue was raised by what has been called colorism. Although affirmative action was often thought to reflect the effort of minority groups to secure rights held by majority, generally white, groups, there could also be within-minority groups discrimination based on racial characteristics. Among the most prominent of these characteristics was the darkness or lightness of the skin color. Like racism itself, colorism was discrimination based on that skin tone. It was said that blacks discriminated against each other more than did any other minority group in the United States. Though still a small number, the Equal Employment Opportunity Commission saw a continuing increase in allegations of discrimination. Further it was noted that, except interestingly for conservative U.S. Supreme Court Justice Clarence Thomas, almost all prominent black leaders in education, the media, government, business, and related fields were light-skinned. An exception occurred in specifically civil rights groups. It was also noted that most African Americans remained unwilling to discuss this issue.

What moral questions are raised by affirmative action?

Among the moral questions raised by the prominent instances of affirmative action were the following. From at least four possibilities, what ought to be done about discrimination? First, stop the discrimination and let matters then take their own course. Two, stop the discrimination and provide for all those who can prove that they have been discriminated against. Three, stop the discrimination and actively help all who are members of the group that has been discriminated against. Four, reverse the discrimination and discriminate against those who had discriminated.

Further questions included these. What ought to be the racial (or linguistic) goals of society? Among the possible goals were the following. Assimilate the minority into the majority, blacks, for example, accepting white standards, the non-English speaking accepting English, and so on. Encourage the minority to remain diverse and to resist assimilation into the majority, blacks retaining whatever differentiates them from whites in language, dress, customs, and so forth; non-English speaking retaining their language and culture. Encourage the majority to tolerate the minority, preferring assimilation over diversity, but remaining tolerant of diversity though not encouraging it. What was true of race and language could as well be true of religion and other important matters in society.

Further questions included these. Did programs of affirmative action have the effect of stigmatizing members of the favored group by suggesting that no one in that favored group could be chosen except by preferential standards? Was it fair to penalize individuals who had no part in past wrongs? Could one's racial, ethnic heritage alone qualify one to be penalized? How did that differ from what happened in the past? Did many of the problems in society stem from class status rather than from race? How long ought the time frame for correcting problems to be? What about African Americans who were really Jamaican Americans or Dominican Americans and who had no connection with Africa and who had only recently arrived in the United States?

What arguments favor affirmative action?

Various kinds of arguments have been made favoring affirmative action programs. Among them are these. They would compensate individuals for past injustices (compensation for past wrongs). They would more equitably distribute income, positions, according to individuals' needs (redistribution of society's goods). The society as a whole would benefit, causing the greatest good to the greatest number of individuals (utilitarian considerations). And, most importantly, especially in education, diversity was a good in and of itself.

Further, authors like Bowen and Bok in their book *The Shape of the River*, and Bok in his own writings, found that blacks who were admitted through affirmative action to selective colleges had higher graduation rates, held more leadership roles in civil organizations, made major contributions to the professions; and their presence on campus had positive effects on civic and social attitudes, and on preparing students for the reality of diverse populations, and did not contribute to stigmatization.

What arguments disfavor affirmative action?

Arguments against affirmative action programs included these. They required the people to shoulder the burden of past wrongs. Those chosen because of it would not be able to perform adequately in the profession, school, or job. Race was irrelevant to many professions, schools, and jobs, and ought not therefore to figure into decisions about acceptance or employment. Those thought to be helped were actually stigmatized by affirmative action. Once race was considered, it could as easily be used to prevent as to assist. Class differences suggested that lower class whites needed help more than upper class blacks. Some research by Harvard professor Robert Putnam suggested that diversity had more short-term drawbacks than benefits to society in terms of social capital. He argued that "in the short run there is a tradeoff between diversity and community." "It would unfortunate if a politically correct progressivism were to deny the reality of the challenge to social solidarity posed by diversity." But then he added: "It would be equally unfortunate if an ahistorical and ethnocentric conservatism were to deny that addressing that challenge is both feasible and desirable."

What conclusions did the U.S. Supreme Court cases reach concerning affirmative action in higher education?

We begin with legal considerations and U.S. Supreme Court cases involving affirmative action in higher education.

We start with the first important case dealing with affirmative action in higher education to reach the U.S. Supreme Court. Although it concerned graduate medical education, its implications went far beyond that narrow focus. In Regents of the University of California v. Bakke, the Supreme Court both approved the concept of affirmative action and ordered him admitted to the medical school which it found had unconstitutionally denied him a place in their entering class. We then turn to two cases involving the University of Michigan, one with its undergraduate admissions procedure and one with its law school admissions procedure.

What was the case of Regents of the University of California v. Bakke?

The 1978 case of Regents of the University of California v. Bakke examined a special admissions program to the Medical School of the University of California at Davis which had reject him under their affirmative action plan.

The facts of the case showed that the medical school had a separate admissions program to increase the number of disadvantaged, a term that was undefined, enrolled in the school. Different cut-off scores were used in that separate program which meant that minority candidates with lower scores could be admitted rather than white candidates with higher scores. Bakke, applying late in the cycle, did not meet the requirements for a white applicant though he ranked higher than black applicants admitted. He protested. He reapplied earlier the following year but his interviewer then (the associate dean to whom he had previously written protesting the separate program) down-scored him because of what the dean termed his lack of understanding. Bakke was again rejected. He sued.

What did that case decide about diversity and affirmative action?

Justice Powell, writing for the majority of the U.S. Supreme Court, ruled that colleges and universities could consider "ethnic diversity" as "only one element in a range of factors a university properly may consider in attaining the goal of a heterogeneous student body." But they could not use a program like Davis' which solely gave specific points to minority candidates. The Court declared that "Preferring members of any one group for no reason other than race or ethnic origin is discrimination for its own sake." Title VI of the Civil Rights Act of 1964, and the Equal Protection Clause of the Fourteenth Amendment to the U.S. Constitution forbid it, he wrote.

In his opinion, Justice Powell referred specifically to the Harvard College program which considered race as but one factor in a mix of factors. That program did not indicate the relative strength of the various economic, talent, geographical, racial, ethnic, and other factors. Its very lack of clarity commended Harvard's program, the Supreme Court seemed to say. Justice Powell accepted the educational value of diversity.

What was a partial dissenting view?

Justice Marshall, who was black, applauded the Court's decision that race could be considered by admissions committees. But he disagreed with other parts of the decision. He wrote that "it must be remembered that, during most of the past 200 years, the Constitution as interpreted by this Court did not prohibit the most ingenious and pervasive forms of discrimination against the Negro. Now, when a State acts to remedy the effects of that legacy of discrimination, I cannot believe that this same Constitution stands as a barrier."

"The position of the Negro today in America is the tragic but inevitable consequence of centuries of unequal treatment. Measured by any benchmark of comfort or achievement, meaningful equality remains a distant dream for the Negro. In light of the sorry history of discrimination and its devastating impact on the lives of Negroes, bringing the Negro into the mainstream of American life should be a state interest of the highest order. To fail to do so is to ensure that America will forever remain a divided society. I do not believe that the Fourteenth Amendment requires us to accept that fate. Neither its history nor our past cases lend any support to the conclusion that a university may not remedy the cumulative effects of society's discrimination by giving consideration to race in an effort to increase the number and percentage of Negro doctors."

What was the aftermath of that decision?

Five years after the Bakke decision, the *Chronicle of Higher Education* reported that the ruling appeared to have had little effect on the proportion of black students in college, especially in medical and law schools; and that Bakke's lawyer said the question raised by the case was: "Are we going to judge people by their color or by the content of their character?" His lawyer emphasized that problems of discrimination had not affected every black person or every white person in the same way.

Ten years after the Bakke decision, in 1988, Bakke was an anesthesiologist in Minnesota, minority students admissions held steady or perhaps increased slightly, and reactions to the Bakke case remained polarized. Supporters of the decision said it was right to allow preferential treatment but acknowledged that admissions depended on a school's own predilections rather than on law. Opponents of the decision said the emphasis on race diminished the importance of merit and led to a decline in academic standards.

Twenty-five years after the Bakke decision, the U.S. Supreme Court reached opposite conclusions in two cases from the University of Michigan, one concerning undergraduate admissions and the other concerning law school admissions, and one Justice, since retired, made a statement about the future of affirmative action.

What were the Gratz v. Bollinger and Grutter v. Bollinger cases?

Both these cases arose from admissions policies at the University of Michigan. And both cases raised the same question: Does the use by the University of Michigan of racial preferences in admissions violate the Equal Protection Clause of the Fourteenth Amendment or Title VI of the Civil Rights Act of 1964? But the answers the U.S. Supreme Court provided in 2003 were directly opposite each other. In the Grutter case, the court permitted the use of race as one of many factors in admissions, other ones being grades, test scores, personal essays, various talents and abilities, legacy status, and recommendations. In the Gratz case, the court prohibited the awarding of extra points to racial minorities solely because they were minorities.

What did the Court rule about the Michigan Law School's use of race in the Grutter v. Bollinger case?

Justice Sandra Day O'Connor wrote for the 5-4 majority that the Michigan Law School's use of race did not violate the Constitution or the Civil Rights Act. She noted that diversity was an important goal as had been stated in the Bakke case and that the School's inquiry into each candidate's possible diversity contributions did not employ a quota system, but rather followed the "highly individualized review of each applicant" that the Bakke case required. Dissenters concluded that the process was in effect a quota system.

On what did a dissenter rely in that case?

Justice Thomas, the sole black Justice, relied on his own personal history and what he considered the stigma that resulted from what he termed affirmative "racial discrimination" in his dissenting opinion declaring the Michigan process unconstitutional.

What did the Court rule about the Michigan undergraduate admission's use of race in the Gratz v. Bollinger case?

Chief Justice William Rehnquist wrote for the 6-3 majority that the Michigan undergraduate admission's use of racial preferences did violate both the Equal Protection Clause and Title VI. The Court agreed that diversity could be a compelling state interest, but it held that the automatic distribution of 20 points out of the 100 needed to guarantee admission, to every underrepresented minority who was African American, Hispanic, or Native American, solely because of race, did not meet the Bakke test of individualized consideration. Twenty-five years after the Bakke case, the University of Michigan was using the very system for considering the race of freshmen applicants to its undergraduate program that the majority in the Bakke case had ruled unconstitutional. Only six of the Justices, however, concluded that that made the program unconstitutional.

How long will affirmative action be necessary?

Justice Sandra Day O'Connor wrote in 2003: "We expect that 25 years from now, the use of racial preferences will no longer be necessary to further the interests approved today."

What was the Michigan Civil Rights Initiative?

Ward Connerly, who had successfully guided a ban on affirmative affirmative action in California in 1996, created the Michigan Civil Rights Initiative with Jennifer Gratz, and in November 2006 approximately 58% of Michigan voters approved a ban on affirmative action in public education, public employment, and state contracts.

What were other related affirmative action issues?

A number of related issues include these, among others. How ought a law review to selected its editors? Ought non-traditional casting to be used? How should racial classifications be determined? What is colorism? How does the U.S. Government use Census data to determine eligibility for affirmative action programs? What are the longer-term benefits of achieving diversity? What are the short-term drawbacks to implementing diversity? What effect does affirmative action admittance have on its recipients? Should there be an end-point to the law's acceptance of affirmative action programs? What do dissident blacks conclude about affirmative action?

Did some advocates for affirmative action suggest that it was applied more often by institutions of higher education to benefit wealthy white youth than black youth?

Two books argued as the subtitle of one stated that "rich white kids are winning the college war over affirmative action" and as the subtitle of the other stated that

"America's ruling class buys its way into elite colleges." Both detailed the influence of money and connections in the admission to elite colleges of youth whose scores and talents were less than others admitted. Neither saw the necessity for colleges that depended on the private donations of wealthy alumni to reward those and future alumni to keep producing further financial support. Neither suggested alternative ways to ensure those donations. Both concluded that those wealthy whites ought to be the target of anti-affirmative action arguments rather than blacks and Hispanics most often considered the recipients of affirmative action.

Following the Regents of the University of California v. Bakke decision, what did law reviews do to expand the diversity of their editors?

In 1995, R. Weisberg reflected on his time at the *Stanford Law Review* some years before and on the process of selecting editors at prestigious law reviews. While the system had for many years been solely grade-related at a place like Harvard, that system produced mostly white men and troubled those concerned with diversity. In his article, Weisberg recounted that editors who were to choose their successors experienced inner conflict. He wrote "that law reviews have only become concerned with affirmative action many years after most law students became deeply interested in the issue's place in society generally and in university hiring and admissions particularly." Further he noted that "Students otherwise committed to deconstructing the traditional, disparity-producing norms of elite meritocracy seem to be very slow to give them up in law reviews." He thought students considered law reviews important either as the last stand against "social redistribution" or as so important to the individual chosen and to society that affirmative action was required in the selection of editors. A brief review of the struggles of the *Harvard Law Review*, after Bakke in 1978 and before Weisberg's review in 1995 and continuing beyond, showed the inability of what was considered the top law review in what was often considered one of the top law schools to reach a plan. If those lawyers-to-be could not plan readily, one might ask, how could the law expect others less-trained, perhaps less-able to accomplish that task?

What difficulties did the Harvard Law Review *face in the years following Bakke in attempting to implement affirmative action?*

One of the top law reviews in one the top law schools in the country showed how difficult implementation of affirmative action plans found constitutional in the Bakke case could be as the *Harvard Law Review* attempted to make a moral decision concerning whom to admit to membership. The *Review,* called the "legal profession's most influential journal," published a number of issues each year with articles and commentaries by law professors, judges, practicing lawyers, and law school students.

In 1980-81, Harvard Law School enrolled approximately 1750 students, of whom 28% were women and 14% were minority. At that time, the *Harvard Law Review* had 11 women, one Asian American, and no black editors. In selecting students for membership on the *Review* a simple method had been used for decades. Until 1968, the *Review* chose all of its members solely on the basis of their grade point averages. That plan had yielded three black editors. Then, in 1968, the choice was widened so that some students were chosen on the basis of their grades and some were chosen on the basis of their anonymous participation in a law-review-type writing competition.

Whatever else these plans did, neither one produced enough minority editors or women editors in the eyes of some of the *Review* members. In February 1981, the *Review* contained only one minority student and less than a dozen women. In the fall term, 1980-81, the *Review* accepted no minorities and three women to become part of its 80 members.

Because of these low numbers of minority and women members the *Review* adopted, in February 1981, an affirmative action plan which would give minority students and women a greater opportunity to become a member of the *Review.* Under the previous plan, the *Review* offered membership to the five students in each of the four sections (each of which contained approximately 125 students and to which the first year students were assigned by chance) with the highest grade point averages at the end of their first year of studies at the law school. It then offered places on the *Review* to 20 students through an anonymous writing competition. Because this plan did not produce many minority or women editors for the *Review,* the editors voted 45 to 39 to adopt an affirmative action plan.

Under that affirmative action plan, the *Review* was to choose the top four students in each section and then to search for the highest ranking minority student among the next 25 highest ranking students in the section. Should the *Review* find no minority student in that group, it was then to choose the highest ranking woman student in that group. The writing competition was to have been unchanged.

After the vote, three editors of the *Review* resigned, calling the affirmative action plan "morally reprehensible." And others sought to reconsider the vote. One editor subsequently withdrew the resignation.

What was the new affirmative action plan?

After discussion of the plan, the *Review* adopted by a vote of 44 to 36 a new affirmative action plan in place of the former one adopted February 4. The new plan retained the part of the previous plan that entailed selecting the four highest ranking students from each of the four sections in the first year. After those sixteen students were chosen on the basis of grades, and another sixteen were chosen on the basis of the anonymous writing competition, a further eight students were to be chosen through a combination of grades, the writing competition, and an optional student statement concerning race and/or sex, and any other special circumstances.

The *Review* said that its plan was built on the need for diversity, retained a merit selection process, and simply broadened the concept of merit to include race and/or sex (minorities/women). The *Review* said that it rejected the quota aspect of the plan.

In adopting the revised plan, the *Review* argued that the previous plan had set quotas, had practiced reverse discrimination, had favored the minorities who had similarly been favored in the past, and stigmatized members chosen through the added procedures. *The Harvard Crimson* student newspaper endorsed the new plan in an editorial.

The *New York Times* discussed the extensive controversy concerning the *Harvard Law Review* affirmative action plan. It said the affirmative action plan was significant because of the preeminent place the *Review* held in the nation; because of the emphasis in law firms, clerkships, and other places, of membership on it; and because the plan was seen as the first one by the *Review* to depart from academic criteria in the choice of editors.

What was reaction to the plan?

Reaction to the *Law Review's* affirmative action plan was mixed, according to the *Times*. It quoted a former Cabinet member and one of the first blacks to be elected to the *Review* as saying that membership on the *Review* must be based only on academic merit; and it quoted the president of the Harvard Black Law Students' Association saying the plan did not go far enough to make the *Review* an open journal where everyone who wanted to write for it could.

Later, the *Times* captioned its summary of the controversy among the editors, "A law review reviews its ethics." And in an editorial, the *Times* wrote: "The cause of affirmative action is thus made the adversary of merit. It should not have to bear such a burden from such a place."

The chairman of a special faculty committee was quoted as saying that the *Law Review* had been the "one place where objective, blind judgment has always been the case." His committee was to examine what effects the new affirmative action plan would have in view of that tradition. Further, his committee was to look at the fact that not many blacks went out for the *Law Review*.

Protests concerning the plan grew in strength. Much negative comment had been occasioned by the *Review's* affirmative action plan. Two resigned members of the *Review* continued to protest. *The Wall Street Journal* and *The New York Times* editors wrote against the plan.

Students arguing for the plan said that the numbers showed that something was unfair at the *Review;* that how the situation developed was less important to them than correcting the situation for those who have significant voices in the determination of the law ought to be more broadly representative than the white males who dominated both the *Review* and the legal establishment. Students arguing against the plan said that what people do ought to count for more than who they are.

In late April the faculty committee asked the *Review* to delay implementing its affirmative action plan for a year. The chairman of the faculty committee said that his committee was not pleased with the *Review's* plan. Although they approved the general principle of affirmative action, he said, they did not like the specific method of the plan.

Further, the faculty committee's report said that the plan was not an effective one because it relied on self-identification of minorities; because anonymity could not be maintained; and because it might damage the status accorded to those chosen for the *Review*. Further, the report said that no other honor at the Law School used race or sex as a factor.

A leader of a woman's group at the Law School said that the plan pitted minorities against women, and a leader of the black students said that rejecting an imperfect plan would leave the situation worse by maintaining the current plan.

What happened next?

Next, the faculty at the Law School voted overwhelmingly to ask the *Review* to postpone implementing its plan for one year. It voted to accept the principle of greater heterogeneity on the *Review* but it felt that another plan ought to be devised. One faculty member moved to have the Law School stay out of the matter to respect the autonomy of the *Review,* but that motion was defeated by a vote of 8 to 21.

Further, the faculty report argued that the cause for "even a well designed affirmative action program at the *Review is* more complex and more questionable than in other contexts, particularly admissions." The *Law Review* then voted 35-26 on May 6 to delay their affirmative action plan for one year.

What other issues were raised by what was termed a "more complex and more questionable" affirmative action plan than in other contexts?

In addition to all the issues already mentioned, a number of other issues were raised by the *Law Review* and Faculty's actions and arguments. Among them were the following. What in the *Law Review* context was similar to and what was different from affirmative action plans in college admissions, governmental hiring programs, or other areas in which affirmative action plans were used? How long should minorities and women be dealt with specially because of underrepresentation or past discrimination or disadvantages? What was the University's real view concerning race and sex discrimination?

Was diversity itself valuable on a law review, in college admissions, in employment, elsewhere? Ought diversity to be elevated to the status of a moral mandate? What was the faculty's input into other affirmative action plans and was there discrepancy between its actions elsewhere and at home? How did the prevailing political climate enter into arguments and votes concerning the principle of affirmative action and the specifics of a plan? How could the students at the Law School whom the faculty and other *Law Review* editors declared to be the top students in one of the top law schools not work out a plan that met the satisfaction of the faculty? What did that very fact say about the selection procedures, or the nature of the task? Was the *Law Review* an honor society or a publishing enterprise and ought there to be different methods of selection depending on what its primary goal was?

What were two striking relations between the Harvard Law Review's plan and the admissions plan at the law school itself?

Finally, two points related the *Review* affirmative action controversy to the larger issue of affirmative action considered generally. First, many faculty opposed the *Review's* plan; yet the *Review's* new plan was almost identical to the Law School's own affirmative action plan for admissions, which was based on Harvard College's plan, the plan which was cited in the U.S. Supreme Court's Bakke decision as a model for affirmative action. Second, there were dissenting views among blacks concerning the idea of affirmative action at the *Law Review* because of how it would affect them. The former Cabinet Secretary mentioned above, who was the third black ever elected to the *Review,* in 1942, said: "Getting elected to the *Law Review* was one of the few times in my life when I felt people were being judged by merit alone, with no other considerations entering in. Any system where people don't make it on the abilities they demonstrate at the moment of selection doesn't fit the purpose of the *Review* as an outstanding legal journal."

Yet, that same individual, as chairman of the Legal Defense Fund of the National Association for the Advancement of Colored People, in response to interview questions put by *The New York Times* in 1981, said he thought that affirmative action and Federal contract compliance programs "have made a start, but we still have a situation where blacks do not have the same opportunities and the same jobs as whites." Further, he said that looking at every institution, "you will find that women are not proportionately represented."

He argued that the "only way you can make businesses help is to place restrictions on them. He suggested that the best way would be to say to a private corporation, I don't care what you do, but when you come in here next year, if you're going to get that $2 billion to build that cruise missile, then you have to have a plan that demonstrates that in the last two years you were able to move your women's employment from 10 percent to 25 percent."

And his final comment concerning affirmative action was: "The one set of tools that have worked reasonably well are those tools developed over the last 15 years which go under the rubric of affirmative action. It resulted in more blacks and more women having opportunities. I think that when it's having the success that it is, it's just wrong to stop and turn the clock back unless you can say that the problem is solved. And I don't think anybody can say that."

He thought that what was best for him was not what was best for others. He wanted acknowledgment as having earned, as he saw it, his honor at the *Law Review*, whatever the numerical representations might be. With others, he argued for numerical representations.

What was the status of the plan six, eight, and twenty-five years after the Regents of the University of California v. Bakke case?

In 1984, over 400 first year law students signed a petition saying they would withhold *Review* access to their grades if the *Review* did not select all editors on the basis of writing rather than grades. In response, the *Law Review* voted to end its controversial policy of selecting some editors solely on the basis of first year grades. Under its new plan, the *Review* chose half its members by grades (counting 70%) and performance in a writing competition (counting 30%) and the other half solely through the writing competition. The Dean of the Law School said at the time that he was not satisfied with the results though he was with the students' effort.

When the writing competition was held later that year, no blacks were admitted to the *Review,* though the affirmative action plan was in effect. A letter writer charged that the black writers in the competition were voted down three (white males) to two (one Asian woman and one black woman).

In 1986, the *Review* debated changing its selection policy to emphasize grades far more than writing ability. While defeating such change, it considered accepting a few students solely on the basis of their first year grades if the total number of applicants failed to meet a preset level. The effort was necessary, many felt, to increase the applicants for editors positions.

In 1977, the *Review* elected its first woman president who later became the campaign manager for the Democratic candidate for the presidency in 1988.

In 2003, the *Law Review* drew fire, according to *The Harvard Crimson*, because the number of women on the *Review* had fallen to its lowest point in a decade. The law school was nearly half women, but only a quarter of the editors were women. So the *Law Review* considered establishing gender-based affirmative action for the first time. But, interestingly enough, the effort was not supported by the three faculty advisers, all women, nor by the female dean of the law school, who said, according to *The Crimson* reporter, "if the *Review* announced an affirmative action policy, it would imply that women could not be accepted based on merit alone." This appeared not much different from the comment of the black former *Law Review* member who had said that affirmative action would jeopardize the legitimacy of blacks on the *Law Review*, who, like him, had been selected without affirmative action. Such reactions raise the question of "whose ox is gored."

Why did another law review change its affirmative action plan?

In 1995, the editorial board of the University of Pennsylvania Law Review changed its selection process to make it harder to determine the role of race or ethnicity in selecting editors. It established requirements for scores on its own two-part test as well as on course grades, but kept those secret so no one could tell who was an affirmative action appointment. The policy only applied to black and Hispanic students. One problem even with the new system was that few black or Hispanic students entered the competition.

What is a strong minority perspective?

When he was elected as the first black president of the *Law Review* in 1990, Barack Obama said that his goal was to "furnish a strong minority perspective." That raised the question of what was either *a* or *the* strong minority perspective. The goal of furnishing it required some consensus whether there was a black (or an Asian or a woman's) view. Usually the dominant black minority perspective was the view held by the acknowledged or self-appointed leaders of the community, by the majority of blacks, and by their liberal white supporters. This black view advocated affirmative action, for example. Those blacks who did not support it were considered disloyal and as not having a "black perspective." It was said they could not help blacks to make the moral decision, or the political or other important decisions. Among those more conservative black thinkers and writers were English Professor Shelby Steele, Law Professor Randall Kennedy, Linguistics Professor John McWhorter, educational activist Ward Connerly, and others.

What were the views of dissenting minorities?

A number of black dissidents argued their alternative view of the causes and cures for underachievement, and the contribution they saw affirmative action making to that problem.

Shelby Steele, in his book *The Content of Our Character*, termed affirmative action a Faustian bargain. He argued that it fostered the myth of black inferiority, and that middle-class values were necessary to prosper academically, vocationally, and in other ways. He termed those values raceless, assimilationist, and mainstream. They included, he contended, the Protestant work ethic, the importance of education, the value of property, ownership, respectability, getting ahead, stable family life, initiative, and self-reliance.

Ward Connerly, in his book *Creating Equal*, fought against race preferences because he argued that they validated blacks' fear of inferiority and reinforced racial stereotypes.

John McWhorter, in his book *Losing the Race*, contended that affirmative action fostered policies of separatism, victimology, and anti-intellectualism.

Randall Kennedy, in his book *Nigger*, strongly challenged the view that there was a unique minority perspective on legal issues, arguing instead that there were a variety of political, cultural and personal ideas held by people of color and that many minority professors and some white liberal law professors did not want the topic of this diversity of viewpoints even to be raised, let alone discussed or advocated. He said they wanted uniformity of view on that matter. And many studies supported his overall view concerning a lack of ideological diversity by showing that whatever the race, ethnicity, or gender of faculty members at the elite colleges and law schools, they were overwhelmingly liberal and Democratic.

Another black professor, Martin Kilson, however, harshly reviewed Kennedy's book. Kilson said that Kennedy was claiming to free up whites by using the attention-getting title word, whereas Kilson contended that Kennedy was a "black-rejectionist" with a view of "African-American ethnic or cultural group patterns as the main obstacle to a colorblind society."

Finally, comedian Bill Cosby said at a National Association for the Advancement of Colored People banquet honoring the 50th anniversary of the U.S. Supreme Court decision in Brown v. Board of Education desegregating public schools that the black lower socioeconomic class use of non-standard English, perpetuation of criminal activity within their neighborhoods, inadequate parenting, and disinterest in education were major contributing factors to their lack of economic and social progress. Criticism of his views focused on what were termed his elitism and classism, and said that his even mentioning such matters contributed to bias and prejudice.

Yet, a documentary filmed for HBO about the 50th anniversary in September 2007 of the tumultuous entrance of black youth into all-white Little Rock Central High School focused on the sharp divide there between white students in Advanced Placement courses and black youth inadequately parented and prepared, lacking motivation, in remedial courses rather than in those Advanced Placement courses. The documentary interviewed individual black and white students, their families, the school's teachers and principal. One of the original youths who were accompanied by federal troops into the school in 1957 returned to a classroom at the school for the documentary and declared that the division was systemically caused. Her view was countered by the mother of a black girl in Advanced Placement courses who insisted that motivation and parenting and the importance of education were too often neglected by blacks in the school. Near its end, the documentary showed two black men setting up markers for those who had died as a result of black-on-black crime in the community. The two men mourned the fact and wondered how to stop it.

Clearly, the arguments between supporters of the dominant and of the dissenting views were heated and the consequences of their implementation significant.

What further issue did a prominent politician's identification as a black person raise?

A decade and a half after his statement, Barack Obama's identification as a black man confirmed one issue and raised another. The son of a white American woman and a black Nigerian man, Obama's identification as black suggested that when the racial mixture was equal, assuming it was, the minority classification outweighed the majority classification. Given the choice between identifying with a black parent and a white parent, Obama chose (or to some extent others chose for him) the black. Though Tiger Woods had invented the term Cablinasian (a combination of Caucasian, black, American-Indian, and Asian) to describe himself, Obama did not attempt to define himself in a way analogous to Woods' self-characterization.

Neither was it suggested that a new term was needed. But the choice also implicitly suggested to some that racial classification ranked higher than national classification. Given the choice between identifying with an American and a

Nigerian, even though he was an American citizen, he chose the Nigerian. Thus, some argued, race trumped even citizenship in the self-identifying choice.

What determines racial classifications?

More basic than minority perspective was racial classification itself. If employment or admission to school were to be based, through affirmative action, on race, how was that to be accomplished? Methods, for example, of determining who was black depended to some extent on the self report of individuals seeking admission or employment. Just as in the past black individuals tried to pass for white to better themselves, it happened with affirmative action that white individuals tried to pass for black in the employment, admissions, and other areas in order to better themselves. What, in fact, had white and black meant?

A Public Broadcasting System documentary referred to the "one-drop rule," which meant that any person with any known African black ancestry would be considered black. In the South that was called the "one-drop rule" or the "one black ancestor rule" or the "traceable amount rule" or the "hypo-descent rule," under which racially mixed persons were assigned the status of the subordinate group.

Carrying the matter of affirmative action to its logical extreme meant that society would have to define race very carefully, specifically, and then everyone would have to be classified according to race, as Louisiana had attempted and as South Africa had done. If the intent were benign, to foster affirmative action, what, some asked, would be wrong with such an approach. Examples illustrated the moral problems.

A 48 year old Louisiana woman, whose birth certificate listed her as black but who had considered herself white, sued to have the 1970 state law that said anyone with 1/32 "Negro blood" was legally black declared unconstitutional. The state traced her genealogy and concluded she was 3/32 black. Her attorney said no one could tell by any scientific test who was black or white. The state said it did not want to classify by race; parents should do that.

Two firefighters in Boston, though apparently white, claimed a black great-grandmother and gained their jobs through affirmative action. Ten years later, both were fired. Another firefighter who claimed Hispanic status on his application was reinstated because he had made a legitimate mistake. He established that one of his great-great-grandfathers had been born in Cuba and the selection committee mistakenly accepted that as proof of minority status. All such cases raised questions of truth in labeling.

A successful candidate for a City Council position listed himself as black because he said that about twenty years before he decided that because he felt black he must be black. His parents listed him as white; he had fair skin and blue eyes. But he said he was black culturally, socially and genetically: "My choice is my choice." The U.S. Government in its census had each person decide his or her own race using whatever criteria the person wanted.

How did the U.S. Census change its system of racial classifications?

The example of the U.S. Census was instructive. Prior to the 2000 Census, each person could self-identify with only one racial classification. As Stephan Thernstrom noted in a conservative publication, that in essence followed the "one-drop still" rule that had prevailed, so that any black ancestry, no matter how small, made the individual black. In fact, in Louisiana, to be one-eighth black was to be black. Even less was often required. But Tiger Woods, as noted, had made his racial status memorable by commenting that he was Cablinasian because of his own ancestral diversity.

The federal government appeared to agree that acknowledging diversity was important. It declared that racial and ethnic categories should not be considered primarily biological or genetic, but rather as a combination of social, cultural, and ancestral characteristics. It allowed an individual to check many racial boxes, not just the one that had been previously required. Tiger Woods could check all the boxes that made up his Cablinasian identity. The traditional civil rights groups, however, objected to this expansion or diffusion of classifications for an individual, because of the fear that it would diminish the number of people who were considered black, bringing therefore less support, less redress of inequality, and less importance for their groups.

How did the Office of Management and Budget change the Census classification system?

But the Office of Management and Budget allayed their fears. It declared that for a number of purposes such as "civil rights monitoring and enforcement" anyone who checked any minority race would be considered to be of that race. Thernstrom contended that that increased the numbers of minority individuals because those in the past who wished to be considered white and checked that classification might thereafter, in an effort to be more open and diverse, acknowledge some black ancestry as well. That, according to the guidelines, made them black for civil rights purposes.

Can whites or others have a black or Hispanic or Asian minority perspective, or a man a woman's perspective?

Many argued that only a minority could successfully have a minority perspective. As an example, when the white longtime executive director of the NAACP Legal Defense Fund, who had argued Brown v. Board of Education and other prominent cases, was to co-teach with the black president of that fund a course at Harvard Law School on racial discrimination and civil rights, minorities boycotted the course. They said that his ideas may have been black, but he was not. Only one black student, a postdoctoral fellow at the Graduate School of Education, took the course. Those who favored a more narrow definition of the minority perspective felt they had made the moral decision. Their opponents did not.

August Wilson, author of the acclaimed play, *Fences,* made his position clear: "I want a black director for the movie." Among the reasons Wilson gave were a shared cultural ground, shared political and economic systems, a rapidly developing ethos, specific ideas and attitudes. In his own words, "I declined a white director not on the basis of race but on the basis of culture."

An Hispanic American author won the American Academy and Institute of Arts and Letters prize for the outstanding work of fiction published during the previous twelve month, a novel about a Mexican American family in a Los Angeles neighborhood. The dust jacket of the book described the author as having grown up in Los Angeles. But the author was not Hispanic American, as the critics and awarders and indeed his own publisher from whom he remained totally hidden, had assumed, but a 73 year old white graduate of Andover and Yale, who majored in classical Greek in college. The author considered his name change and false biographical status to be a "mild deception." He and his wife had done volunteer work for twenty years in the Los Angeles barrio. His use of a Hispanic name was both denounced and defended.

The chairman of the seven-member American Committee that voted the award said the new information about the author cast a different light on the matter. "We were considering the ethnic dimension. If we had known, it would have given us pause. We would not necessarily have rejected it, but we would have had to talk a little more about it. It does raise all kind of interesting questions."

Can someone who had not lived a certain experience write about it or play the role on stage or in film?

Many wrote or acted who have not lived the experience they addressed, raising many questions. Why have writers in the past, like Mark Twain or George Eliot, used pen names? By using a minority pen name, was the writer trying to be published as a minority writer when he might not have been able to as a white writer? What were the advantages to anyone of renaming himself? Was the deception intentional or a byproduct of some more benign motive? Should a literary or other work be judged by the work itself or by the political or ethnic or racial orientation of the author? What happened to, or should have happened to, writers when their real names were revealed?

Issues with authors also concerned actors. Could someone who was white play the role of a minority? It was important to note that there had long been such casting, and that blacks often sought to play roles originally written for whites. There had always been instances of color blind casting, called nontraditional casting, or in Britain integrated casting. Whites played blacks and other minorities. Sir Lawrence Olivier played Othello; Elizabeth Taylor, Cleopatra; Rudolph Nureyev, the King. Blacks played whites. Morgan Freeman played Petruchio; Pearl Bailey, Dolly Levi; Denzel Washington, Richard III; Robert Guillaume, the Phantom.

But when the producer of *Miss Saigon* planned more than a decade ago to bring the award winning white actor Jonathan Pryce to New York to recreate his role of the Eurasian Engineer, Actor's Equity denied his casting. The union, at the request of two prominent men of Asian ancestry, playwright David Henry Hwang and actor B.D. Wong, agreed that there were too few parts for Asians and other minorities and that when a part came along no actor other than an Asian ought to get the part. The union explicitly said it had made a moral decision aimed at creating equal casting opportunities for its minority members.

Mr. Mackintosh, the producer of the show, asked if Equity would also condemn a black, such as Morgan Freeman, portraying a white, such as Petruchio, "or is American Equity's concept of equal racial equality a one-way street designed to curb the very heart of the actor's craft?" He argued that because Equity rejected Mr. Pryce solely because the actor was Caucasian, the union had engaged in discrimination.

Mr. Pryce said, "It has to be seen as an illegal and unconstitutional act to deny me employment because of my race. They would have to just come right out and say that they were wrong." Finally, Mr. Pryce noted that the Engineer was Eurasian and that unless the actor himself were Eurasian he would have "to drop down on one side of the fence or the other and I'm choosing to drop down on the European side." He and others wondered whether creativity could be mandated by affirmative action requirements.

Rather than compromise his artistic freedom, he said, Mr. Mackintosh cancelled the Broadway production of his multimillion dollar show. Actor's Equity quickly reversed itself, at that point saying it had "applied an honest and moral principle in an inappropriate manner." Mr. Mackintosh met with the union to discuss issues and announced the production's arrival on Broadway. Basic economic realities seemed to have triumphed over the initial moral objection of the union.

A final interesting note: Hwang's award winning play, *M. Butterfly,* featured B.D. Wong as a man who disguised himself as a woman to have a two decade long affair with a man whose child he had. Many commentators pointed to this incongruous element in the Hwang/Wong challenge to Jonathan Pryce's portrayal of a Eurasian, and raised a question. When the conflict seemed to be between artistic freedom and equal employment opportunity or affirmative action, which decision really was the moral one?

Sometime later, a prominent black female author took an opposing view, considering a person's ideas and approaches more important than his actual race. She said she considered Bill Clinton the first black president.

In responding to a criminal justice situation, what was meant by "acting like he's white"?

In September 2007, black activist Jesse Jackson sharply criticized presidential hopeful and Illinois Senator Barack Obama for "acting like he's white" in what Jackson said had been a weak response to the arrest of six black juveniles on attempted-murder charges in Louisiana. Yet that comment recalled to many people Jackson's statement in 1993. Then he said: "There is nothing more painful for me at this stage in my life than to walk down the street and hear footsteps … and then look around and see somebody white and feel relieved."

What did a black economist and his colleague mean by "acting white"?

In their article in *The Quarterly Journal of Economics,* black economist Roland Fryer and his colleague referred to what they called "the social price paid by the best and brightest minority students." In a brief explanation of the phrase, they said that "acting white" was "a set of social interactions in which minority adolescents who get good grades in school enjoy less social popularity than white students who do well academically."

What was the "mismatch" effect?

The research of a UCLA law professor focused on what he concluded was the academic price paid because of a "mismatch" effect. In an article in the *Stanford Law Review* Richard Sander wrote that several thousand underprepared black students who were admitted because of affirmative action to law schools for which they were unqualified dropped out or did not pass the bar examination. He and his research team maintained that if those students had instead attended schools which were less competitive and therefore more matched to their own abilities, more of them would have graduated, passed bar exams, and become lawyers.

Was controversy often a staple of nontraditional decisions?

Controversy has always followed nontraditional decisions. When the design of Maya Lin, an Asian ancestry student at Yale, was chosen to design the Washington, D.C. Vietnam Memorial her ethnicity raised great protest. That her memorial became a highly praised, emotionally fulfilling, triumphant work suggested to many that the art work itself ought to be judged, not the artist who produced it.

But that turn of events did not stop black protest about the artist chosen to sculpt Martin Luther King, Jr. for the Washington, D.C. Mall. He was denounced by black activists as a Chinese non-citizen who ought not to have been chosen to portray such a prominent black man. The memorial foundation in charge of the project was startled by the criticism because ten of the twelve committee members who chose the sculptor were black, and a black-owned architectural firm directed it. Also the foundation planned to feature King's words saying that people must "transcend race, our tribe, our class, and our nation" to "develop a world perspective." Further, the president of the foundation noted King's words that people should be judged by the content of character rather than by the color of skin. Of course, when the black scholar Shelby Steele noted that in the title of his anti-affirmative action book, *The Content of Our Character*, he was denounced by mainstream black leaders as an Uncle Tom and a virtual traitor to his race.

How does language itself contribute to bias?

As many have noted, the biases in our very language contribute to implicit, if not explicit, biases in society. The word black prefacing days of the week, for example, almost always signaled loss or disaster. Black Thursday (October 24, 1929) referred to the start of the stock market crash and the Great Depression and was followed by Black Monday and Black Tuesday (the 28th and 29th). Black Monday (October 19, 1987) referred to the extraordinary drop in the Dow Jones Industrial Average. Often referring to monetary disasters as these, the only generally positive use of such a characterization accompanied Black Friday (the day after Thanksgiving), originally perhaps referring to the busy purchasing, but more recently to the fact that the intake from customers put stores into the black (an accounting positive) instead of into the red (an accounting negative). Words have reverberations, as even this brief list suggests.

Finally, Webster's definitions in the *Third New International Dictionary* illustrated this widespread factor. Some of the definitions of white included these: free from blemish, moral stain, or impurity; righteous; innocent; decent. Some of the definitions of black included these: wicked; dishonorable; hostile; unqualified; illicit; illegal. Because language informs perspective it helps to explain deep biases and the basis for continuing implicit if not explicit stereotypes. Even the use of his when referring to either a male or female, as has been the practice, duplicated even in these pages, connotes something which makes many readers uncomfortable, as does the repeated use of his or her, or the use of the plural their with the singular of one person. Language sometimes does not readily support changing views or aspirations.

8

Professional Conduct

What ethical problems arise in the conduct of professionals?

The legal and moral issues of professionals within the Roman Catholic and Christian Science faiths have already been addressed in the chapter on the care of children. Here, two specific examples from the legal profession, one from the medical profession, and one from the education profession raise interesting issues about legal and moral decision making.

Often the word ethical is applied to the moral conduct of professionals. In fact, one of the prominent definitions of ethical forms it with the example of an ethical lawyer. But what makes an ethical lawyer? Clearly, being fiscally honest, dealing with clients and courts truthfully are attributes of an ethical lawyer, as is following the professional code of ethics about confidentiality and related matters. But who is to decide what makes a lawyer unethical? And who is to decide what happens if an unethical lawyer who has been disbarred, for example, rehabilitates himself and wants to be readmitted to practice? What does the profession understand to be society's view of the ethics of the legal or the medical, or other profession?

The moral problems involved in professional conduct concern the obligations of the professional in law, psychiatry and psychology, education, divinity, and elsewhere toward the profession itself, toward clients, patients, students, and toward the general public. Many of these obligations are set forth in professional codes of ethics. But what about those ethical standards which clearly violate normal ethical or moral standards? When professions deviate from those normal standards, on the theory that they are helping their clients and society, but with the fact that they are sometimes more helping themselves, how are those deviations to be evaluated?

Additional issues raised by professional conduct include the following. What are the limits of moral conduct? By what standards ought professionals' conduct to be judged? How much consensus is there about standards and how much dispute? What are the kinds of sanctions available for immoral and/or illegal conduct? How are those applied? How should they be applied? Why are they or are they not applied?

And the final question in this section is equally an important question for all the sections. How varying are the views concerning this moral problem? And how much do the experts, those affected by the problem more specifically, and the general public agree among themselves or disagree concerning both the nature of the moral problem and of making the moral decision?

What determines whether a disbarred lawyer has the moral fitness for reinstatement to the practice of law?

We begin with materials concerning Richard Gordon, a lawyer and judge who was convicted of a criminal charge and sentenced to prison. His conduct was both unethical and illegal. He was disbarred. Nearly two decades later, he sought reinstatement to the bar. Four decisions show the moral decision making which impacted the outcome of his appeal. The first decision was a prior one by the Massachusetts Supreme Judicial Court in the case of disbarred lawyer Alger Hiss who sought reinstatement some years after his prison sentence. That case was later cited in Gordon's case. The second was by the Massachusetts Board of Bar Overseers, whose function was to supervise and discipline lawyers and who, after conducting hearings, considered Gordon to be morally fit to be reinstated to the bar. The third was by the Bar Counsel who independently recommended that Gordon not be reinstated. And the fourth was by the Massachusetts Supreme Judicial Court which had ultimate authority and which did not heed the Board of Bar Overseers conclusions, did accord with an independent Bar Counsel, and decided not to reinstate him to membership in the Bar.

Was a disbarred and imprisoned lawyer sufficiently rehabilitated to be reinstated?

In 1952, Alger Hiss was disbarred after his 1950 conviction on two counts of perjury in testimony before a Federal grand jury. The case was a celebrated one because of the involvement of the Committee on UnAmerican Activities of the

House of Representatives. Hiss served three and a half years in prison. He never admitted guilt. In 1974, 69 year old Hiss petitioned for reinstatement as an attorney. The Board of Bar Overseers heard evidence and filed a report answering three questions. First, were the crimes so serious that Hiss ought never to be reinstated as a lawyer? Second, were recognition of guilt and statements of repentance required for reinstatement? Third, was Hiss at the time of his petition fit to practice law in Massachusetts?

Chief Justice Tauro in his opinion noted that "Hiss comes before us now as a convicted perjurer, whose crime, a direct and reprehensible attack on the foundations of our judicial system, is further tainted by the breach of confidence and trust which underlay his conviction. His conviction and subsequent disbarment are 'conclusive evidence of his lack of moral character at the time of his removal from office.'"

Tauro further noted that the majority "cannot subscribe to the arguments advanced by the chief Bar Counsel that, because the offenses committed by Hiss are so serious, they forever bar reinstatement irrespective of good conduct or reform." That position, Tauro said, assumed that such individuals were "incapable of meaningful reform." That position he declared "is foreign to our system of reasonable, merciful justice." And he said that a statement of repentance and an acknowledgment of adjudicated guilt were not requirements for reinstatement. Rather, "To satisfy the requirements of present good moral character in the tests for reinstatement, it is sufficient that the petitioner adduce substantial proof that he has such an appreciation of the distinctions between right and wrong in the conduct of men toward each other as will make him a fit and safe person to engage in the practice of law." This was because the Court recognized "that a convicted person may on sincere reasoning believe himself to be innocent."

Further, the Court declared Hiss fit to serve as an attorney based on his character, conduct since disbarment, time elapsed, and present legal skills. It acknowledged that the Board of Bar Overseers found Hiss at the time of his petition "of good moral character," that the passage of 23 years was sufficient time, and that he was gainfully employed. The opinion concluded by noting that "The board could correctly find that Hiss has sustained the heavy burden of showing moral and intellectual fitness by good and sufficient proofs." The opinion also concluded that he would be competent enough as a lawyer. The court granted his petition for reinstatement to the bar.

Under similar circumstances, why was a different disbarred and imprisoned lawyer refused readmission?

In 1965, as a result of his conviction of April 16, 1963 of larceny, a felony, and conspiracy to commit larceny, a misdemeanor, in connection with the construction of the Boston Common Underground Garage, Richard Gordon was convicted and sentenced to prison. At the time he had been a lawyer and a Special Justice in a state district court. He served almost three years in prison. In 1978, the 58 year old Gordon petitioned for reinstatement to the bar. The Board of Bar Overseers investigated the matter. It held a hearing. It received letters from a range of people interested in his reinstatement; a petition with over 700 signatures; articles, other documents, and letters; and testimony from several individuals, including this author who knew him and the family through his son who had been in my course, worked as my teaching assistant, and was the sponsor of a weekly seminar I conducted at Yale for a number of years.

The Board concluded that Gordon met his burden of showing "that he has the moral qualifications, competency and learning in the law" to be reinstated and "that his resumption of the practice of law will not be detrimental to the integrity and standing of the bar, the administration of justice, or to the public interest, and recommends that Gordon be reinstated to the bar of the Commonwealth." Since his release from prison Gordon was first a bookkeeper and then a self-employed tax consultant. In an odd twist, though he did not say he was a lawyer, he did "practice before the United States Tax Court, from which he was not disbarred."

The Board suggested that it might be advisable to require him to engage in some continuing education. Beyond that the Board found "Gordon morally qualified at this time to be a member of the bar" even though he was a judge at the time of the offenses. They cited the Hiss case concerning rehabilitation, the lack of necessity to admit guilt, and the requirements for reinstatement, and noted that Gordon's criminal conduct did not relate to his judicial duties.

They concluded: "The final factor that we must consider is the effect of Gordon's reinstatement on the standing and integrity of the bar, the administration of justice, and the public welfare. Neither the Criminal Court nor the Attorney General nor the Massachusetts Bar Association has offered any opposition to the present petition. Moreover, the Essex Bar Association has gone on record as favoring Gordon's reinstatement. Equally important is the absence of evidence of any other public opposition to Gordon's reinstatement or evidence that such reinstatement would give rise to any adverse reaction among the bar or the public. On the contrary, on the basis of testimony of residents of Gordon's community concerning public opinion on the issue, it appears that his reinstatement would be well received by many members of the bar and public." The Board recommended his reinstatement.

The independent Bar Counsel also investigated the matter. The Bar Counsel argued that the court had to look behind subjective testimonials as to the present good character of the petitioner "to the public record of the conduct which caused the disbarment in the first place." That led the Bar Counsel to recommend against his reinstatement.

In the majority opinion of the Massachusetts Supreme Judicial Court, Chief Justice Hennessey wrote: "We conclude that Gordon should not be reinstated." The Court evidently considered "larcenies and corruption relating to public funds" to be more serious than perjury was in the Hiss case. And it considered public opinion to be more unforgiving in the Gordon matter than it was in the Hiss matter. In subsequently discussing this issue in classes, many more there knew of Hiss and that matter than knew of Gordon and this matter. It appeared that it was the Justices of the Supreme Court who thought of themselves as the remembering public, rather than the 700 who signed the petition and others who found the public more forgiving.

The Court said it had "given respect and close attention to the conclusions of the Board of Bar Overseers" but it did not follow their recommendation because the Court concluded that "public perception of a reinstatement of Gordon at this time would in high probability reflect badly upon the reputation of the bar for integrity." Rather than base its conclusion on a poll or other survey, the Court determined its own reaction to the reinstatement and so ruled.

Justice Lynch wrote in his concurring opinion: "I share the concern expressed in the dissent, however, that the result reached here appears inconsistent with Matter of Hiss. To the extent that a disparity exists between the treatment of Gordon and Hiss, I believe that the course we follow here is the correct one."

In a dissenting opinion, Justice Nolan wrote: "In 1975, this court unanimously granted the petition for reinstatement of an unrepentant but convicted perjurer in spite of an adverse recommendation by the Board of Bar Overseers in Matter of Hiss. In this case, the Board of Bar Overseers recommends the reinstatement of Gordon, but the court denies his petition."

He continued: "In trying to gauge the impact of Gordon's readmission to the bar on the public, the court reminds us of the scandal of the Boston Common

Garage cases and describes them as 'a notorious saga of corruption and theft.' However, by comparison with the national controversy of the Hiss trial, Gordon's prosecution was only a local media attraction. Gordon's conduct for which he was convicted was reprehensible and all the more so because he was a judge at the time, but, to his credit, he does not remain obdurate and unregenerate while protesting his innocence. I find it most difficult to understand the reason for the difference in treatment between Hiss and Gordon.

I would allow Gordon's petition for reinstatement on condition that he pass the Massachusetts bar examination."

Five years after he petitioned for reinstatement, Richard Gordon appeared on Attorney F. Lee Bailey's television program, *Lie Detector* where he was examined by a polygraph expert, who reported his results on the program. Attorney Bailey concluded, "There isn't any question that in his own mind, Mr. Gordon has told the truth." Mr. Gordon felt cleared by the results of the test as far as his own original conviction was concerned. Two defense lawyers also appeared on the program to present their view that Mr. Gordon was innocent of the charges of which he was convicted.

How were the actions of the prosecutor in the Duke lacrosse case both unethical and illegal?

In the next case, the lawyer, a District Attorney, was found in 2007 to have violated legal ethics and to have broken the law. He was removed from his elected post as a North Carolina District Attorney, disbarred as an attorney, and briefly jailed. In addition, the victims of his unethical and illegal behavior sued him and others. The case was widely publicized and a book about it, *Until Proven Innocent*, attacked both the District Attorney's unethical and illegal behavior and the unethical behavior of the President of and Faculty members at Duke University.

Michael Nifong was in a tight electoral race. A Duke lacrosse team party gave him the opportunity to rally black voters to vote for him. The team hired two strippers to perform at their party. As events unfolded, one of the women later said she had been raped at the party. Subsequent investigation by defense lawyers revealed that Nifong had employed a completely faulty line-up to determine who the rapists were, had made statements in defiance of legal ethics, had withheld crucial exculpatory DNA evidence from the defense, and had lied to the court about what he had done and not done. When all that was made clear, the state Attorney General cleared the three players charged with rape; the North Carolina Bar Association Board considered the evidence against Nifong, and disbarred him; and the judge held Nifong in contempt for lying to him and ordered him briefly jailed.

The Nifong case, once the facts were known, was a straightforward one. Nifong acted in violation of legal ethics and he violated the law. As many commentators suggested, however, his case was unusual in that a district attorney was held accountable for his behavior. Too often, those commentators said, public prosecutors who engaged in similar unethical, even illegal behavior, were not held to account, except by the voters, who as in the Duke lacrosse case might consider the actions to benefit them regardless of illegality or lack of ethics.

What was the unethical behavior of the President and members of the faculty of Duke University?

The authors of *Until Proven Innocent* focused some of their scathing criticism on the President of Duke University, Richard Brodhead, and members of his faculty. At the outset, Brodhead denounced the team, fired the coach, dismantled the team, and terminated the season. As Abigail Thernstrom reported in the *Wall Street Journal*, Brodhead "condemned the lacrosse players as if they had already been found guilty" and ignored the increasing evidence that the players were innocent. Further, over eighty Duke faculty members signed a statement which, while reacting to general campus feelings about racism, sexism, and related topics, appeared to condemn the Duke lacrosse players who were white for their conduct toward the black women they had hired to entertain at their party. More specifically, according to *The Chronicle of Higher Education*, a literature professor Wahneema Lubiano wrote that the lacrosse players were "almost perfect offenders" as they were "the exemplars of the upper end of the class hierarchy, the politically dominant race and ethnicity, the dominant gender, the dominant sexuality, and the dominant social group on campus." And according to *The Chronicle* another professor, Houston Baker, had written the Provost demanding that the University immediately dismiss the students and coaches because of their "abhorrent sexual assault, verbal racial violence, and drunken, white male privilege loosed amongst us." Neither they nor the others retracted their virulent comments, nor did those who sought castration, or otherwise threatened the players, even after the players were fully cleared.

After the three defendants were completely exonerated and the District Attorney disbarred and jailed, the so-called Group of 88 posted an online letter in which they defended themselves against accusations that they had rushed to judge the players guilty. In their letter they refused to retract their initial statement or to apologize. The authors of the book *Until Proven Innocent* found that a reprehensible example of what they termed the climate of political correctness at celebrated educational institutions such as Duke.

What was the motive for the Duke President's unethical behavior?

The book authors theorized that Brodhead acted out of concern for himself. They said he feared that if he did not denounce the students the faculty might turn on him as faculty at Harvard had turned on their President, Lawrence Summers, after he questioned a black professor's scholarship for producing a rap CD and refused tenure to a black woman whose research centered on hip hop; and then raised the issue for research of whether women's underrepresentation in science had something to do with them as women. Brodhead might have had reason to worry, the authors suggested. Subsequent events at Harvard showed the danger of anti-political-correctness behavior. Summers was removed as President and the woman selected as his successor soon offered tenure to the black female hip hop scholar, and pledged to expand black faculty and staff numbers dramatically. Summers refused comment on the matter.

A further development involving former President Summers showed the continuing danger of not following the political correctness of the prevailing faculty view. In September 2007, the *Chronicle of Higher Education* reported that the Board of Regents of the University of California withdrew a speaking invitation to Summers after a petition drive by female faculty members on the campus nearest where the board was to meet gathered 350 signatures. Those faculty said having Summers speak was not appropriate especially since the University was attempting to add diversity to its faculty. They felt nothing he had to say could rehabilitate him. He remained to them a symbol of gender and racial prejudice. The Regents invited the female chief of staff to the Governor to be the speaker instead.

The Nifong, Duke President and faculty incident raised questions of ethical behavior in both law and education, and of unlawful behavior in law. Whether Nifong at some point in the future would seek reinstatement to the bar remained unknown. The President of Duke retained his position despite what many criticized as his disregard for basic fairness and the rule of law.

Did the President of Duke University apologize for his own conduct in the lacrosse case?

The Duke President eventually did apologize, but not until September 29, months after the North Carolina Attorney General had declared the three defendants not guilty, and even after the District Attorney had been disbarred, convicted, and sentenced to jail. The timing suggested that he was forced to apologize then only because a book condemning his and some Duke faculty's actions had been published the day before. That book, *Until Proven Innocent*, called his and others' behavior on the Duke campus shameful. While his apology was greeted by applause, it appeared to many still to demonstrate inadequate recognition of his and many of his faculty member's unethical conduct. Those faculty, the so-called Duke 88, who condemned the accused, never did apologize, nor did the President admonish them, nor were they censured, nor were they chastised by the administration of the University. The subtitle of Taylor and Johnson's book appeared substantiated by the events before the dismissal of the charges, and after as well.

Did the three former Duke lacrosse players falsely accused of rape file a federal civil lawsuit?

The three falsely accused former Duke lacrosse players filed a suit for compensatory and punitive damages against the city of Durham, NC, the disbarred and briefly imprisoned former District Attorney Michael Nifong, the former police chief and several police detectives and officers, and they made several suggestions for future police conduct.

Why did a writer criticize the President of Columbia University, who was the President of Michigan when the affirmative action cases arose there, for his behavior concerning debate, reason, and homosexuals?

A writer for the *Wall Street Journal* pointed out the incongruity between two actions of the former president of the University of Michigan, whose name appeared on the Gratz and Grutter Supreme Court cases concerning affirmative action there. On the one hand, the writer said, Bollinger invited the President of Iran to speak at Columbia with an introduction by Bollinger who was then president there, as part of "Columbia's long-standing tradition of serving as a major forum for robust debate." in an effort Bollinger said to encourage listening to others' viewpoints. And a Dean there said they would also have invited Hitler to speak there.

On the other hand, the writer said, Bollinger joined faculty in preventing the presence of the Reserve Officers Training Corps on campus because of its "don't ask, don't tell" policy concerning homosexuals and the military. Yet the writer noted that the military policy that the University decried was far less serious than the penalty for homosexuals that Human Rights Watch found in Iran. Human Rights Watch reported that Iran's Shariah-based penal code set the punishment for all penetrative sexual acts between adult men as the death penalty, and for all non-penetrative acts between men and for all sexual acts between women as lashes through the fourth offense and then with death. The writer, in effect, questioned the sincerity, wisdom, and moral basis of Bollinger's stated belief in "robust debate" in opening the campus to the President of Iran but not to the ROTC.

What ethical issue arose in an educational and medical context over letters of recommendation?

Professional conduct arises in many different forms. The lawyers in the Hiss and Gordon cases were disbarred and sought reinstatement as individuals capable of being ethical members of their professions. One was reinstated and one was not. Among doctors, there many opportunities arise for unethical behavior. More common matters involve their direct practice of medicine and we will address that shortly. A less obvious way in which they make moral choices concern the writing of letters of recommendation, when they decide whether they will expose their immoral or incompetent colleagues. Even though it may seem clear to the public that doctors should expose them, the codes of silence which seem to influence some in all professions appear to be established in medicine as elsewhere. Some doctors cover up, as have priests and others, because they felt that their profession's credibility with the public demanded their silence about unethical conduct within the profession, or considered matters to be borderline, or did not want to involve themselves, or worried about privacy, or preferred to handle matters more surreptitiously than directly.

The next case, from some years back, illustrated these issues, in the context of the added concern of serious sexual harassment, assault. An anesthesiologist at a major Harvard Medical School teaching hospital in Boston was charged, along with two other doctors, with rape. He was convicted by a jury of raping a nurse from the hospital, after a party, at the parents' home of one of the doctors. Sentenced to prison for the rape, he appealed the conviction and was freed pending the appeal. Placed on leave of absence by the hospital, he disappeared from sight.

Subsequently, he was charged with the rape of one women and attempted rape of another woman at a different hospital some time prior to the rape of the nurse from the Boston hospital. At that time he was a staff member of the suburban hospital and the two women were patients there. Located by the police in another state, where he was employed as an anesthesiologist at a children's hospital, he was returned to Boston.

The ethical issue arose from letters of recommendation written for him by three prominent staff members of the Boston hospital. After his conviction for rape, the doctor asked the chief of anesthesiology at the Boston hospital who was also a professor at the Harvard Medical School, as well as two other doctors at the hospital, to write him letters of recommendation. All three wrote letters for him on Harvard Medical School/official hospital stationery. None of the three mentioned his conviction for rape nor any of the circumstances of his leaving the Boston hospital. All praised him as an extraordinarily fine anesthesiologist. The out-of-state children's hospital relied on the letters and characterized them as completely laudatory and as giving no suggestion of any difficulty in his life. The children's hospital relied on the stature of the doctors who wrote the letters and on their affiliation with Harvard Medical School, prominently displayed on the stationery, and hired the doctor, not realizing or suspecting his conviction. It was only when the local police there came to the hospital to arrest him that the children's hospital became aware of his past.

What was the reaction to the recommenders' behavior?

Reaction to the incident was strong. *The Boston Globe* editorialized that the recommenders had perhaps not considered the conviction for a crime to be actually that, that they might have considered that a doctor who had sexual relations with a nurse after a party actually had not raped that nurse, no matter what she said and a jury believed. *The Globe* suggested that the case raised issues of the nature of rape, the power structure within the medical profession, the urge of the profession to protect its own, the willingness of important professionals to lie at least indirectly, and the general attitude of damning the public by arrogant medical doctors.

Further, it appeared that the recommenders did not follow the American Medical Association's Principles of Medical Ethics which stated: "The medical profession should safeguard the public and itself against physicians deficient in moral character or professional competence. They should expose without hesitation illegal or unethical conduct of fellow members of the profession."

In letters to the editor, one woman noted that business people would not write such a letter on their own firm's stationery, let alone on Harvard Medical School stationery. She also added, "The bottom line here, as always, is that no woman is going to interrupt a doctor's career. The arrogance is astonishing."

Another woman wrote that she found it incredible that Harvard Medical School faculty could write glowing letters of recommendation for a doctor after he had been convicted of rape, a vicious crime of hostility against women, and sentenced to prison. "Such action by these people seems to reflect at the highest level the indifference to and contempt for the most basic wellbeing of women by the masculine medical community."

A male doctor wrote of his outrage that any doctor, but especially a doctor at a teaching hospital, would write a recommendation for a doctor after he had been convicted of rape: "What has happened to the medical ethic that held character, integrity and responsibility as the hallmarks of our profession? Technical ability and knowledge are important for one to be a good physician, but they are secondary to those essential qualities of character that allow people to put their lives in our hands."

Finally, the Dean of the Harvard Medical School raised general questions about such letters: "When preparing references, to what extent and under what circumstances should a member of the Faculty volunteer information about personal behavior away from the work place? What kinds of previous actions should always be reported to potential future employers because they suggest that the candidate lacks the capability to accept ethical responsibility? When does the volunteering of information become an invasion of the personal privacy of the candidate?"

What is the relation between competence and malpractice?

The next case raised the issue of competence in the medical profession and its relation to moral decision making. Whether a physician who caused physical harm to a patient was acting unethically depended to some extent on where the line was drawn between competence and malpractice. While the line was not clear cut and lawyers could advocate on their client's behalf that the line might be drawn in various places for various purposes, it seemed evident that the line signaling malpractice was extremely low. The case demonstrated that much very poor practice was not considered malpractice by other doctors, and what was true of doctors was true of members of other professions as well. What, then, was substandard behavior in law, medicine, journalism? How far below substandard was behavior that could be termed malpractice? Were, for example, routine unnecessary tests or even operations part of the average practice of medicine, the substandard practice, or did they constitute medical malpractice?

The issues were raised by a presentation on the investigative program *60 Minutes*. The program, reported by Ed Bradley, focused on a neurosurgeon practicing at a suburban Massachusetts hospital. The emphasis in the program was on the inability of the Licensing Board in Massachusetts to keep track of medical negligence of physicians in the state. The title of the program, broadcast in the mid 1980s, "Who Examines the Doctor?" captured the inquiry the program was making. In pointing out the defects in the Massachusetts Licensing Board, *60 Minutes* focused on one neurosurgeon. Over an eight year period, nearly one third of all money paid out against Massachusetts neurosurgeons by the state's lending insurance company was paid in cases involving that neurosurgeon, yet, according to the program, there was no record of that fact in the state licensing board.

What was the case of the malpracticing suburban neurosurgeon?

The program detailed the treatment of a woman who became legally blind and the matter was settled for $600,000; of someone who had become paralyzed and the case was settled for $200,000 and the records of the settlement impounded by the court; and of the case where the harmed person was warned by the court to remain silent about the settlement and the doctor, or risk losing all the money. Over seven years, there was one jury settlement against the neurosurgeon, four out of court settlements, and approximately $2 million was paid out by the insurer, according to the program.

One issue the program raised involved the state's inability to monitor, or examine, doctors through its licensing board. A part of that issue was the matter of secrecy, the requirement by courts that those hurt remained silent if they were to receive their money. Another issue involved the standard of treatment. Interviewed by Mr. Bradley, the neurosurgeon said, "I am a superb neurosurgeon." The chief at another elite medical school, commenting on one of the cases, said the treatment involved a negligent recommendation; it was not legitimate. A professor of neurosurgery at still another elite medical school testified that in one case the operation was useless and fraught with hazard and he doubted that a good doctor would advise the same procedure, but the insurance company settled before the neurosurgeon's doctor had a chance to testify. The insurance company paid $900,000 in the settlement. Mr. Bradley asked the neurosurgeon if he considered himself guilty of substandard care. The neurosurgeon replied, "absolutely no." In fact, the neurosurgeon said that seven chiefs of neurosurgery, at his request, had reviewed the cases and had found no malpractice on his part. Mr. Bradley acknowledged that.

In commenting on the entire matter, the chief of neurosurgery at an elite medical center said that the neurosurgeon was average; he said he probably had a problem with his judgment, probably some of his work was ill-advised and injudicious and unnecessary. But that chief of neurosurgery said that many physicians routinely performed operations that were not necessary. Those were therefore part of the average care and could not be considered malpractice. The chief of neurosurgery added that he saw inappropriate treatment day in and day out which was not malpractice.

The program concluded with the question of whether the licensing board should review these kinds of cases, especially where there were multiple occurrences. Mr. Bradley noted that not once in 1983 or 1984 did the Massachusetts licensing board take action against any of the 17,000 physicians in the Commonwealth for medical negligence. As illustrated in the *60 Minutes* program, there was, in addition to the burden of inadequate or poor practice of medicine that fell below the acceptable level but did not reach the malpractice level, the burden of silence, the silence of doctors, the silence of hospitals, the silence imposed by courts on settlements.

What changes were made in Massachusetts and elsewhere?

That silence ended, to some extent, on September 1, 1990. At that time the National Practitioner Data Bank began collecting information on medical malpractice. The data bank included information on doctors, dentists, psychotherapists, and other licensed healthcare practitioners; medical licenses, hospital privileges or society memberships which were suspended for 30 days or more; and malpractice settlements and resignations which took place after an investigation has begun. The system expected to record 60,000 reports each year; of these 40,000 would record payments in medical malpractice settlements or judgments. Doctors could review their own files and write rebuttals. At its inception, access to the data bank was limited to official regulatory groups like state licensing boards, hospital peer review boards, and professional societies. Consumer advocacy groups urged the opening of the data bank to the general public as well.

Were such a data bank in operation at the time of the rapist-doctor's crime or the neurosurgeon's malpractice, both would have been recorded and those with official authorization would have had access to the data bank. Whatever the results of such a data bank, consumer groups advocated careful compiling of information, broad public access to the information, and wide use of the information in making healthcare and professional decisions.

What subsequently occurred to inform the public of a doctor's record of malpractice?

In 1996, Massachusetts became the first state to require physician profiles and in 1997, placed those profiles on the Internet. In addition to basic information about training and related matters, the profiles reported any malpractice actions against a doctor within the past ten years.

What happened to the suburban neurosurgeon in the years after that program?

The neurosurgeon's record indicated no malpractice actions against him for the past ten years. Further, he became a leading figure in professional organizations, elected to executive positions.

How do competence and ethics relate to each other in professional practice?

Taking the matter of malpractice one step further, there remained the additional issue of competence in relation to ethical practice. A few years after the program aired, that suburban neurosurgeon was assigned to my mother who was visiting when her developing spinal problem required immediate surgery. He was the one who was assigned to operate on her back. Upon learning of his involvement and the impending surgery, I consulted with colleagues at the Harvard Medical School and with medical doctors at leading Boston hospitals and made arrangements for her to be transferred to one of the major Harvard Medical School teaching hospitals in Boston.

Needless to say, I had made a thorough canvass to assure her a high level of professional skill. She was scheduled to be operated on by a thoroughly competent physician. On the night before the operation, that Boston neurosurgeon visited her in the hospital room where she and I were talking.

He began to speak to her about the high cost of medical practice in Massachusetts, the artificial limits placed by insurance on the medical charges he could make, the unfairness of the Medicare cap, the fact, he said, that it was driving most of the able practitioners out of Massachusetts, and the importance of his work and research. She listened quietly. He then recited the mandatory list of possible serious harmful outcomes of such an operation. Though somewhat rare, he said, they constituted an impressive, and to her somewhat frightening list. Upon concluding that listing he asked her whether she would contribute $3,000 to his research fund. While his tone was gentle and he seemed to be making a simple inquiry, its placement in the context of the risks involved in the surgery, the complication because of her earlier scheduled operation with the suburban neurosurgeon, and her general debilitated condition occasioned some concern on her part. She was uncertain what to say and turned to me. I, too, realized all these factors, and thought it best to agree at that time and then decide later what to do about the situation. She signed nothing, saying whatever the Boston neurosurgeon thought best would be fine with her.

The operation proceeded successfully. The Boston neurosurgeon was extremely competent. I then called a number of Harvard Medical School faculty to discuss the situation, to raise the ethical issues involved in the request and its timing, and to inquire about the context of caps on fees, research funds, and related topics. The next day, after the operation, the neurosurgeon gave my mother a card with only his name on it, without his M.D. designation, and asked her to write a check to be paid directly to him. There was no indication of a research fund on the card he gave her or in the instructions for the check.

Doctors with whom I consulted declared his behavior to be unethical. But they were divided as to what should be done about the situation, beyond not paying the amount, citing problems with proof, accuracy, and punishment. While the concern with the suburban neurosurgeon had been about his level of competence, the Boston neurosurgeon performed extremely competently, but appeared to be unethical. When discussing the matter with my mother, she said that as between competence and ethics, when they seemed to be in conflict, she would choose competence.

I thought carefully about what to do next and then acted on others' advice and my own view of the entire situation.

How can one know whether a lawyer, as in earlier cases, or a physician, as in this case, was rehabilitated?

One further odd coincidence occurred with the suburban neurosurgeon and it raised the question of rehabilitation. I fractured my femur while trying to shovel a very light coating of snow off thick driveway ice. Taken to the same hospital my mother had initially entered, an extremely competent and completely ethical orthopedic surgeon there repaired the fracture. When sometime after that, a disk herniated, I consulted with him about whether or not to have surgery. He gave me for consultation the names of two neurosurgeons, one the very doctor who had been featured on *60 Minutes* and from whose pending operation on her I had removed my mother, and the other a doctor at the medical center where the chief of neurosurgery was the one who had commented in the *60 Minutes* broadcast. Imagine my surprise. Recalling that the suburban neurosurgeon's performance had been termed average or substandard or in a number of instances evidence of malpractice, and also that he had had no instances of malpractice judgments in the last ten years and that he had attained a number of profession-related positions, I hesitated while considering the matter with the orthopedic surgeon. Of course, the issue raised more considerations that simply the matter of rehabilitation, but certainly held a place of some importance in determining which one to turn to for consultation and possible operation. The important question was raised. To what extent was rehabilitation possible, and even if it was, to what extent would the lingering effect of the earlier malpractice and substandard care be influential in a decision some years later?

9

Sexual Conduct

What is the moral and legal problem?

This material on the general topic of sexual conduct focuses first on consensual same-sex behavior and then on nonconsensual sexual harassment. Both topics raise moral and legal questions. The first case, Bowers v. Hardwick, involved sexual morality in terms of homosexual behavior, specifically homosexual sodomy. In it, the U.S. Supreme Court ruled that state laws criminalizing homosexual sodomy were constitutional. A decade and a half later, the case of Lawrence and Garner v. Texas overruled Hardwick finding those laws unconstitutional. Before turning to those cases, this chapter presents background material on psychiatric diagnoses and on different ways of conceptualizing sexual orientation.

What was the timeline concerning psychiatric diagnoses of homosexuality?

Until 1973, the official classification of the American Psychiatric Association, the *Diagnostic and Statistical Manual of Mental Disorders,* considered homosexuality a mental disorder. In 1973, as a result of political activism, detailed later in the book *Homosexuality and American Psychiatry*, the *Manual* reclassified homosexuality. It was not per se a mental disorder, only one if the homosexual individual found it to be ego dystonic (not in accord with the self) rather than ego syntonic (in accord). In 1986, the Supreme Court decided the case of Bowers v. Hardwick, examined below. In 1987, the *Manual* again reclassified homosexuality, declaring that it was not a mental disorder, even if ego dystonic.

In 1989, the *Harvard Law Review* published an extensive Note on *Sexual Orientation and the Law*, explained below. In 1990, one of the majority justices in the Bowers case revealed later information that helped explain his decision in that case. In 1991, the Harvard publication *Peninsula* condemned homosexuality and

Harvard's Plummer Professor of Christian Morals who was also the Pusey Minister in Harvard's Memorial Church declared at a rally denouncing *Peninsula* that he was Christian and homosexual. In 2003, the U.S. Supreme Court decided Lawrence and Garner. In overturning Bowers v. Hardwick it ruled that anti-homosexual-sodomy laws were unconstitutional. And in that same year the Massachusetts Supreme Judicial Court interpreted the Massachusetts Constitution and ruled in Goodridge v. Department of Public Health that same-sex marriage was constitutional. Massachusetts since then was the only state in which it was legal. Many other states, through a variety of laws, declared it illegal.

What four ways of thinking about sexual orientation were contained in much of the law and policy concerning homosexuals?

In 1990, the *Harvard Law Review* Note *Sexual Orientation and the Law* presented four ways of thinking about sexual orientation that it said were contained in much of the law and policy concerning homosexuals. The Note stated, "One or more of these views underlies the statutes, regulations and case law." The four views were termed sin, sickness, neutral difference, and social construct. Each of them was explained in the Note.

The first, sin, often followed a religious orientation and considered homosexuality to be immoral and wrong.

The second, sickness, took a psychological/psychiatric view. It formerly considered homosexuality to be a mental disorder; then it considered it to be a mental disorder only if it were an orientation unwanted by the person (so called ego dystonic homosexuality); and at the time of the Note it did not consider it to be a mental disorder at all.

The third, neutral difference, suggested that homosexuality was simply a different orientation and attached no value judgment to that difference.

And the fourth, social construct, rejected even the category of homosexuality, viewing sexual acts as interchangeable, whoever happened to be involved in them.

The stated purpose of the *Harvard Law Review* book containing the Note was to discuss "the viability of legal theories supporting the rights of lesbians and gay men." Included within it were a number of comments on the case of Bowers v. Hardwick.

What was the case of Bowers v. Hardwick?

In 1982, because of a mix-up by the court concerning what date Michael Hardwick was to appear there as a result of his violation of the open container law in Georgia, he did now show up when they thought he would. So a police officer went to Hardwick's apartment and was invited in by another person there who told him Hardwick was in the back of the apartment. When the police officer entered that room, Hardwick and another man were engaging in sexual behavior illegal in Georgia. Their oral/anal sex violated a statute which made such behavior illegal whoever was involved. Hardwick was charged with the crime of sodomy. Later, in an interview, Hardwick said he was sure that if the officer had seen a man and woman engaging in the same behavior, also illegal under the Georgia statute, the officer would have excused himself and not charged them. Once the court's mix-up was discovered, the district attorney decided not to present the matter to the grand jury. At that point, advocacy groups approached Hardwick asking him to become a test case, because the advocates for homosexual rights wanted the Georgia law ruled unconstitutional. The punishment for the offense of sodomy was imprisonment for not less than one year nor more than 20 years. Though his going forward with the case put him in some jeopardy of prison, Hardwick agreed.

What did the U.S. Supreme Court rule in Bowers v Hardwick?

In 1986, Justice White wrote the majority opinion for the Court. He concluded that the state sodomy statute did not violate the fundamental constitutional rights of homosexuals. He said the court was not deciding if those kinds of laws were "wise or desirable," and that state legislatures could repeal their laws if they chose to, or state courts could invalidate those laws on state constitutional grounds. He wrote that "The issue presented is whether the Federal Constitution confers a fundamental right upon homosexuals to engage in sodomy and hence invalidates the laws of the many states that still make such conduct illegal and have done so for a very long time. The case also calls for some judgment about the limits of the court's role in carrying out its constitutional mandate."

White began by registering disagreement "that the Court's prior cases have construed the Constitution to confer a right of privacy that extends to homosexual sodomy and for all intents and purposes have decided this case." Further, he stated that the previous cases did not "stand for the proposition that any kind of private sexual conduct between consenting adults is constitutionally insulated from state prescription."

He then referred, as originalists would, to ancient history, to common law, to the original 13 states, to the ratification of the Fourteenth Amendment, and to the practice by states of outlawing such behavior. None of his reasons referred explicitly to religious or philosophical or other value systems, though the "ancient roots" referred implicitly to them. Rather, he said: "Proscriptions against that conduct have ancient roots. Sodomy was a criminal offense at common law and was forbidden by the laws of the original 13 states when they ratified the Bill of Rights. In 1868, when the 14th Amendment was ratified, all but 5 of the 37 states in the Union had criminal sodomy laws. In fact, until 1961, all 50 states outlawed sodomy, and today, 24 states and the District of Columbia continue to provide criminal penalties for sodomy performed in private between consenting adults. Against this background, to claim that a right to engage in such conduct is 'deeply rooted in this nation's history and tradition' or 'implicit in the concept of ordered liberty' is, at best, facetious."

"Nor are we," he said, "inclined to take a more expansive view of our authority to discover new fundamental rights imbedded in the Due Process Clause. The Court is most vulnerable and comes nearest illegitimacy when it deals with judge-made constitutional law having little or no recognizable roots in the language or design of the Constitution."

These reasons were similar to the ones he raised in dissenting in the Roe v. Wade declaring anti-abortion statutes unconstitutional.

Justice White also argued that it would be difficult to limit legalization to consensual homosexual behavior while leaving illegal such sexual behavior as adultery, incest, and other sexual crimes, and as a consequence, a start should not be made.

Finally, Justice White dismissed the Hardwick argument that the only basis for the Georgia law was the belief of a majority "that homosexual sodomy is immoral and unacceptable," and that that rationale was inadequate. White wrote: "The law, however, is constantly based on notions of morality, and if all laws representing essentially moral choices are to be invalidated under the Due Process Clause, the courts will be very busy indeed."

On what basis did the Chief Justice concur in that case?

Justice Burger specifically referred to a number of religious, philosophical, political, and legal bases for his agreeing with the majority decision in the case. They included Judeo-Christian moral standards, Roman and English law, the extremely strong commentaries of the English legal writer Blackstone, and the history of ecclesiastical courts as well as of Georgia legislation.

He wrote: "As the Court notes, the proscriptions against sodomy have very 'ancient roots.' Decisions of individuals relating to homosexual conduct have been subject to state intervention throughout the history of Western civilization. Condemnation of those practices is firmly rooted in Judeo-Christian moral and ethical standards. Homosexual sodomy was a capital crime under Roman law. During the English Reformation when powers of the ecclesiastical courts were transferred to the King's Courts, the first English statute criminalizing sodomy was passed. Blackstone described 'the infamous crime against nature' as an offense of 'deeper malignity' than rape, a heinous act 'the very mention of which is a disgrace to human nature,' and 'crime not fit to be named.' The common law of England, including its prohibition of sodomy, became the received law of Georgia and other colonies. In 1816 the Georgia Legislature passed the statute at issue here, and the statute has been continuously in force in one form or another since that time. To hold that the act of homosexual sodomy is somehow protected as a fundamental right would be to cast aside millennia of moral teaching."

He continued: "This is essentially not a question of personal 'preferences' but rather of the legislative authority of the state. I find nothing in the Constitution depriving a state of the power to enact the statute challenged here."

What argument did a concurring opinion raise?

Justice Powell said that the possible sentence of up to 20 years for a single, consensual act of sodomy, privately, in one's own home, might violate the Eighth Amendment to the Constitution prohibiting cruel or unusual punishment but that because Hardwick "has not been tried, much less convicted and sentenced," that constitutional argument was not before the court. So Powell joined the majority in finding the Georgia laws constitutional.

On what basis did a dissenting opinion consider the law unconstitutional?

In his dissent, Justice Blackmun reframed the question in the case. "This case is not about a 'fundamental right to engage in homosexual sodomy,' as the court proposes to declare. Rather, this case is about 'the most comprehensive of rights and the most valued by civilized men,' namely, 'the right to be let alone.'" He thought the case was about the right to privacy and regardless of the fact that the "moral judgments expressed by statutes may be 'natural and familiar ought not to conclude our judgment upon the question whether statutes embodying them conflict with the Constitution of the United States.'" He considered the right to privacy in this case comparable to the right to privacy in Roe v. Wade.

He further criticized the majority for its "almost obsessive focus on homosexual activity" because the statute covered both it and heterosexual activity. And he disagreed with Georgia's contention that their law was an effort "to maintain a decent society," and with the majority's view "that the fact that the acts described 'for hundreds of years, if not thousands, have been uniformly condemned as immoral' is a sufficient reason to permit a state to ban them today." Blackmun did not consider length of time nor the "assertion that 'traditional Judeo-Christian values proscribe' the conduct involved,'" as providing sufficient rationale for the majority view.

He wrote: "That certain but by no means all, religious groups condemn the behavior at issue gives the State no license to impose their judgments on the entire citizenry. The legitimacy of secular legislation depends instead on whether the State can advance some justification for its law beyond its conformity to religious doctrine. Thus, far from buttressing his case, petitioner's invocation of Leviticus, Romans, St. Thomas Aquinas, and sodomy's heretical status during the Middle Ages undermines his suggestion that the law represents a legitimate use of secular coercive power. A state can no more punish private behavior because religious intolerance than it can punish such behavior because of racial animus."

And further: "Reasonable people may differ whether particular sexual acts are moral or immoral, but Petitioner and the Court fail to see the difference between laws that protect public sensibilities and those that enforce private morality."

Was the Chief Justice's view not a question of his personal preferences?

When Justice Burger wrote "This is essentially not a question of personal preferences," his personal preferences appeared to be extremely clear. He approached the issue of homosexuality from a traditional Christian religious point of view. He condemned it and he was horrified by it. His writing was strong. Condemnation, he wrote, was firmly rooted in Judeo-Christian moral and ethical standards. His personal preferences were especially clear when he quoted approvingly Blackstone's charged words including those about homosexual behavior as more malignant than rape.

What differences about moral standards were there between the majority and the dissenting opinions?

Setting Justice Blackmun's argument against Justice Burger's, it was obvious that Burger assumed the Constitution reflected one set of acceptable moral standards, while Blackmun recognized diverse sets of acceptable moral standards. Burger encouraged condemnation, while Blackmun urged toleration. In many respects the two opinions demonstrated the way in which the Constitution was interpreted as strongly felt personal, religious, moral views shaped the responses of Justices to issues before them.

At the time of the decision in Bowers v. Hardwick, a sample of maximum penalties for sodomy ranged from a $200 fine only for homosexual sodomy in Texas to 20 years for either homosexual or heterosexual sodomy in both Georgia and Rhode Island, and included a number of penalties of severity in between those in a total of 25 states.

In a national poll following the decision in Bowers v. Hardwick, 73% of the respondents knew of the case, 47% disapproved of it and 41% approved; 57% felt homosexuals should be free from such restrictive laws and 74% felt heterosexuals should be subject to them.

What was one concurring Justice's later comment about his decision in the Bowers v. Hardwick case?

At the time of the court's ruling in Bowers v. Hardwick, Justice Powell told other justices that in his 78 years he had never even met a homosexual. And he told that to a clerk who was quietly homosexual and who said nothing about that to Justice Powell. Initially Justice Powell decided to vote to overturn the sodomy laws, but then changed his mind, joining the majority. Some years later he called his vote a mistake and said his view at the time of the case was that it was essentially frivolous because Hardwick was never prosecuted.

What was the Attorney General's behavior at the time he was prosecuting the Bowers v. Hardwick case?

Some time after the Hardwick case, it became known that while Attorney General Bowers was prosecuting Michael Hardwick, Bowers was in the midst of a ten year adulterous affair with an office employee. And at that time, Georgia law also made adultery a crime. So, while Bowers prosecuted Hardwick for violating a Georgia law about sexual behavior, he was himself violating another Georgia law about sexual behavior.

What was the case of Lawrence v. Texas?

In facts similar to those in Bowers v. Hardwick, though as a result of a reported weapons disturbance rather than a missed court appearance for an open container violation, Texas police entered the apartment of John Lawrence, where he and Tyrone Garner were engaging in sexual behavior forbidden by Texas statute. Because Texas law criminalized same-sex sodomy, but not the heterosexual equivalent, the case raised the question of equal protection under the Fourteenth Amendment as well as interests in liberty and privacy under the Due Process Clause of that Amendment. The ultimate question was whether the Court should overrule Bowers v. Hardwick.

What did the Supreme Court decide in Lawrence v. Texas?

The Court ruled that the Texas statute violated the liberty and privacy interests under the Due Process Clause of the Fourteenth Amendment, and that Bowers v. Hardwick should be overruled.

In writing for the majority, Justice Kennedy dismissed what he called the over-statement concerning historical grounds for the law in the Hardwick case. But he acknowledged the ethical and moral attitudes embodied there.

He wrote: "It must be acknowledged, of course, that the Court in Bowers was making the broader point that for centuries there have been powerful voices to condemn homosexual conduct as immoral. The condemnation has been shaped by religious beliefs, conceptions of right and acceptable behavior, and respect for the traditional family. For many persons these are not trivial concerns but profound and deep convictions accepted as ethical and moral principles." But he continued: The issue is whether the majority may use the power of the State to enforce these views on the whole society through the operation of the criminal law."

Next, he referred directly to Justice Burger's concurring opinion in Bowers with its strong views quoted and commented on above. Justice Kennedy referred to the last half century's laws and said they increasingly gave "substantial protection to adult persons in deciding how to conduct their private lives in matters pertaining to sex." He included the American Law Institute's Model Penal Code as evidence of this emergent view. After examining a great deal of other relevant legal and ethical and moral material, Justice Kennedy concluded: "Bowers was not correct when it was decided, and it is not correct today." This Lawrence and Garner case overruled Bowers. By the time it happened, Michael Hardwick had died of AIDS-related illness at the age of 37.

What did a concurring justice say about moral disapproval of homosexuality?

In her concurring opinion, Justice O'Connor wrote: "Moral disapproval of a group cannot be a legitimate governmental interest under the Equal Protection Clause." She agreed that "Texas' sodomy law banning 'deviate sexual intercourse' between consenting adults of the same sex, but not between consenting adults of different sexes, is unconstitutional."

What did the dissent conclude about stare decisis?

Justice Scalia expressed his surprise at the Court's readiness to overrule a "decision rendered a mere 17 years ago." His view was that the principle demanded longer adherence to the precedents of previously decided cases.

What did the dissent conclude about morality?

Justice Scalia said that in overruling Bowers, the Court expressed disinterest in Texas citizens' belief in the immorality of homosexual behavior, but noted that Texas citizens also believed in the immorality and illegality of "bigamy, adultery, adult incest, bestiality, and obscenity." "This effectively decrees the end of all morals legislation." This case, he added, "leaves on pretty shaky grounds state laws limiting marriage to opposite-sex couples."

As for homosexuals and the legal profession, Justice Scalia wrote: "Today's opinion is the product of a Court, which is the product of a law-professional culture, that has largely signed on to the so-called homosexual agenda, by which I mean the agenda promoted by some homosexual activists directed at eliminating the moral opprobrium that has traditionally attached to homosexual conduct."

Lest anyone think anything about Justice Scalia's personal view, he wrote: "Let me be clear that I have nothing against homosexuals, or any other group, promoting their agenda through democratic means."

What was the difference between being a Justice on the Supreme Court and a member of the Texas legislature?

Justice Thomas said, in his dissent, that he found the statute "uncommonly silly," and that as a member of the Texas legislature he would have voted to repeal the statute. But, he said, as a member of the Supreme Court, he voted to uphold the statute: "as a member of this Court I am not empowered to help petitioners and others similarly situated."

What did Lawrence v. Texas suggest concerning stare decisis?

The Lawrence case showed the same readiness to overrule a relatively recent Supreme Court decision that the Gideon case did. Both majority opinions considered the original decisions, in Betts in the one and in Bowers in the other, to have been decided erroneously and therefore considered the overruling not a matter of overturning a precedent so much as correcting a serious mistake which had been allowed to stand for a decade and a half.

What was a dissenter's cautionary conclusion about courts' carrying matters to their logical extreme?

Justice Scalia wrote: "One of the benefits of leaving regulation of this matter to the people rather than to the courts is that the people, unlike judges, need not carry things to their logical conclusion." Justice Scalia expressed his concern that the logical conclusion would be the approval of same-sex marriage. That, of course, was the conclusion that the Massachusetts Supreme Judicial Court reached.

Did the Massachusetts Supreme Judicial Court refer specifically to Lawrence v. Texas when ruling same-sex marriage legal under the Massachusetts state constitution?

In its 2003 decision in Goodridge v. Department of Public Health, the Massachusetts Supreme Judicial Court ruled same-sex marriage legal in the state. In her majority opinion, Chief Justice Margaret Marshall referred directly to "moral and ethical convictions" which were found on both sides of the debate. She wrote: "Many people hold deep-seated religious, moral, and ethical convictions that marriage should be limited to the union of one man and one woman, and that homosexual conduct is immoral. Many hold equally strong religious, moral, and ethical convictions that same-sex couples are entitled to be married and that homosexual persons should be treated no differently than their heterosexual neighbors. Neither view answers the question before us."

In her statement, she, writing for the court, took a rights-oriented position on the question of same-sex marriage, rather than a utilitarian-oriented position. The latter position, information for which could have been gathered by polls, or through Legislative hearings, or in other ways, would have assessed, among other things, how many held each view, rather than simply referring to the fact that many held each view.

But the majority dismissed that distinction, referring instead to the Massachusetts Constitution, and quoting directly (condensed here) from Lawrence v. Texas: "'Our obligation is to define the liberty of all, not to mandate our own moral code.' Lawrence v. Texas (2003), quoting from Planned Parenthood of Southeastern Pa. v. Casey (1992)."

She wrote further that in the Lawrence case, the U.S. Supreme Court "affirmed that the core concept of common human dignity protected by the Fourteenth Amendment to the United States Constitution precludes government intrusion into the deeply personal realms of consensual adult expressions of intimacy and one's choice of an intimate partner." "The Massachusetts Constitution is, if anything, more protective of individual liberty and equality than the Federal Constitution."

What argument did the dissent raise in the Goodridge v. Department of Public Health case?

The dissent interpreted the Massachusetts Constitution differently. It declared that "the marriage statute, as historically interpreted to mean the union of one man and one woman, does not violate the Massachusetts Constitution because 'the Legislature could rationally conclude that it furthers the legitimate State purpose of ensuring, promoting, and supporting an optimal social structure for the bearing and raising of children.'"

No other State Supreme Court interpreted its Constitution in the way the Supreme Judicial Court in Massachusetts interpreted the Massachusetts Constitution.

To what extent did the rights-based view of morality prevail over the utilitarian-based view of morality?

Where homosexual conduct was concerned, the U.S. Supreme Court ruled for a rights-based view of morality, declaring laws against homosexual behavior to be unconstitutional. Where marriage was concerned, the U.S. Congress, as well as many state legislatures, maintained a utilitarian-based view of morality, declaring marriage officially as the union of one man and one woman. Only Massachusetts maintained a rights-based view of the morality of same-sex marriage.

10

Privacy

What is the moral decision about the right to privacy?

Whether privacy involves life and death matters as in issues surrounding the right to die, abortion, or the care of children; or more administrative matters as in issues surrounding the confidentiality of doctor-patient communications, or the search by adopted persons to find their birth parents; privacy remains a central moral problem in contemporary society, one in which individuals attempt to make the distinction between right and wrong in conduct or character. Privacy figures centrally in that attempt. By whatever standard the right or good is defined, religious, philosophical, or legal, privacy is thought to be both a moral and a legal problem.

Does the word privacy appear in the U.S. Constitution?

The word privacy does not appear in the Constitution. Nonetheless, privacy has played a prominent role in judicial and citizen thinking since its first appearance in 1890 in the *Harvard Law Review*. There, an article by Samuel Warren and Louis Brandeis argued for the right to privacy, "the right to be let alone." That article maintained its influence throughout legal as well as moral decision making. In prominent U.S. Supreme Court decisions, the concept and the article were cited favorably by either the majority or dissenting opinions depending on their view of what the outcome of the case should be. More than a century after the article appeared, the legal confirmation hearings of both Judge Bork and Judge Souter turned to a large extent on their differing answers to the question of whether the unenumerated right to privacy was indeed Constitutionally protected. Their declared view or implied view led to the rejection of Bork and the confirmation of Souter.

What did the Harvard Law Review *article say about the right to privacy?*

While their examples seem limited now over a century after their article appeared, their argument maintained its force during that time. They drew their examples from "instantaneous photographs" and "the daily papers" and "numerous mechanical devices," which allowed, for example, "the unauthorized circulation of portraits of private persons and the evil of invasion of privacy by the newspapers."

But their general principle remained the same: "The common law secures to each individual the right of determining, ordinarily, to what extent his thoughts, sentiments, and emotions shall be communicated to others." That protection extends, they argued, "to the personal appearance, sayings, acts, and to personal relation, domestic or otherwise."

And they addressed "the limitations of this right to privacy." They cautioned: "To determine in advance of experience the exact line at which the dignity and convenience of the individual must yield to the demands of the public welfare or private justice would be a difficult task."

It is in the context of the difficulty of the task of determining that line that arguments arise about both the extent and limitations of the right to privacy.

How was the right to privacy featured in the legal cases in this book?

The issue of the right to privacy was featured in a number of U.S. Supreme Court decisions. In this book, the issue found prominence in the cases of Roe v. Wade; Bowers v. Hardwick; Lawrence v. Texas; Washington v. Glucksberg; Cruzan v. Director, Missouri Department of Health; Gonzales v. Oregon; and Vacco v. Quill. What was most interesting about its appearance in these cases was the inconsistency in its application. In some instances, the right to privacy was triumphant and individuals were found to have the right to engage in behavior some or many in society disapproved of. In other instances, the right to privacy was invoked by the dissenters, who argued that individuals who were denied it by law should have the right to engage in that behavior. Because of the lack of consistency in the application to human behaviors of the right to privacy, the cases seemed to indicate that something beyond the right to privacy was involved in highly-charged human dramas.

The majority in Roe v. Wade relied on it to uphold a woman's right to an abortion. The dissent in Bowers v. Hardwick relied on it to condemn the Court's upholding a Georgia law illegalizing consensual homosexual sodomy. The dissent in the Cruzan case relied on it to criticize the Court's refusal to let her parents stop her tube feeding. Lawyers argued that privacy in the family meant that parents could determine the treatment, as well as the upbringing, discipline, and general care of their children free from interference.

What other arguments were made for the importance of privacy?

Rape victims argued that privacy should protect them from mention when the media covered their cases. Professors argued that privacy should protect them from mention when universities disciplined them for sexual harassment. Private clubs and organizations argued that privacy should permit them to exclude women or blacks if they wished. Lawyers and priests argued that the duty of confidentiality to clients or patients outweighed the damage to potential victims or to society itself.

What did professional codes of ethics include about lawyers' requirement for maintaining the privacy of clients?

Professional codes of ethics required lawyers, and doctors and priests, to maintain the confidentiality of their professional communications with clients, patients, and what have been called penitents. The theory underlying this practice was that it encouraged clients, patients, and penitents to seek professional assistance. On balance, that theory concluded that greater good overrode any harm that might result from the privacy requirement.

Privacy was said to be important in lawyer-client situations, for example, for a number of reasons. A lawyer who learned of a client's potential wrong-doing could counsel the client, often successfully, against it. If lawyers did not have a duty of confidentiality, clients would be unable to separate out what to tell their lawyers and what not because they might not understand the full implications of the law. The constitutional requirement of full assistance of counsel could be implemented only by full disclosure. Self-incrimination might occur if the lawyer failed to respect the confidentiality of communication.

While morality might underlie the confidentiality duty, some argued, however, that because lawyers deal in moral ambiguities, they preferred to see the issues in pragmatic rather than moral terms. Those pragmatic terms included such matters as what would enhance their ability to represent their clients; what would make the adversary system of justice function more effectively as an adversary system; what would make clients seek out lawyers if their confidences were not respected.

The requirement of professional privacy has not been absolute, however. While doctors, for example, must maintain the confidentiality of their patients' communications, the California Supreme Court ruled in 1976 in Tarasoff v. Regents of the University of California that health professionals had a duty to warn third parties when they knew or should have known that their patient was dangerous toward such third party or parties. That duty to warn superseded any right to confidentiality the patient might otherwise have enjoyed. The professional was required to invade the patients' right of privacy to protect the safety of another.

Those who advocated wide respect for privacy would make such exceptions for professionals narrow; those who felt privacy must give way to the other social goals would argue for still further limitations on the right to privacy.

What did new technologies contribute to the concern about privacy?

Beyond Warren and Brandeis' concern with newspapers, photos, and other means of communication in the late 1800s, computers have dramatically increased concern about privacy.

Computers made it possible for employers, law enforcement agencies, marketing specialists, interested persons, and others to gather vaster quantities of information on employees, suspected potential offenders, customers, persons at large, and citizens in general. The capacity of computerized data banks to communicate with one another made invasions of privacy much easier to accomplish. Some argued that no new ethical questions were raised by the use of computers, for their only advantages over older methods of information collection were speed and comprehensiveness. Others argued that the opportunities for invasion of privacy were much greater so the effort to maintain privacy in the face of this greater capacity must be greater as well.

Besides this right to privacy, increasing use of computers raised other issues including the right against self-incrimination and the presumption of innocence that the technology of computers helped to diminish. To help maintain privacy, many advocated procedures such as the right to see and correct information, restrictions on dissemination of information, and the use of written consent forms. Supporters of privacy concluded that vigilance remained necessary.

What was the Privacy Act of 1974?

That privacy act governed agencies' use of personal records and required that agencies (but not courts or executive or non-agency parts of the government) keep those records private. But exceptions were made for the Census, and for law enforcement, and for other administrative purposes.

What was the Patriot Act of 2001?

The official name of the USA Patriot Act of 2001 was "Uniting and Strengthening America by providing appropriate tools required to intercept and obstruct terrorism." Its stated mission was "To deter and punish terrorist acts in the United States and around the world, to enhance law enforcement investigatory tools, and for other purposes."

Federal judge Michael Mukasey, nominated to replace Attorney General Gonzales, wrote that many "announced that they will not cooperate with any effort to gather evidence under the statute. A former vice president has called for the statute's repeal, and a former presidential candidate has called the act 'morally wrong,' 'shameful,' and 'unconstitutional.'" They objected primarily with its "investigative techniques, including electronic surveillance and the gathering of business records." Mukasey argued that that opening of surveillance actually extended to new forms of communication permissions that had been granted older forms of communication, and he gave examples of its usefulness in drug and terror and related matters.

Mukasey further argued for support of the statute, especially because it broke "down the wall that has separated intelligence gathering from criminal investigation." Finally, he agreed with the historian Walter Berns who contended that "the built-in message—the hidden message in the structure of the Constitution—is that the government it establishes is entitled, at least in the first instance, to receive from its citizens the benefit of the doubt."

What efforts by the Department of Homeland Security raised privacy concerns?

The Automated Targeting System, in use since the mid-1990s to screen passengers entering the United States, greatly expanded the automation and data collected since 2002, and planned to retain records for fifteen years, in some instances for forty years. The data, obtained from a wide variety of sources, included individuals' traveling companions, places they stayed, books or other personal items they carried with them, and similar kinds of information.

Civil libertarians argued that the government's ability to invade privacy amounted to "a surveillance society," which might at some point limit individuals' right to travel.

The Department of Homeland Security maintained that it mitigated the privacy risks associated with the data collection. Among those risks, the Department said, were possible inaccuracies in the information collected, later misuse of the information, or a negative action in reliance on information "skewed by inaccurate data." Addressing some of the risks separately, the Department concluded that the "system was developed so that the rules are building risk assessments based on the most accurate information available in the source systems."

Others and the Identity Project, which said it "explores and defends the fundamental American right to move freely around our country and to live without constantly having to prove who we are or why we are here," nonetheless raised serious alarm about the privacy invasions. Despite objections, the collection of data continued.

How comparable was the use of cameras and computers to observe citizens in the United States and in the United Kingdom?

While the American Civil Liberties Union questioned police reliance on technology to replace traditional police work when Boston, with a total of 25 cameras, decided to add some of them to observe high-crime neighborhoods, the use of such surveillance in the United States was much more limited than in the United Kingdom. There, a report in the fall of 2007 said that "Britain has a staggering

4.2 million CCTV cameras—one for every 14 people in the country—and 20 per cent of cameras globally. It has been calculated that each person is caught on camera an average of 300 times daily." Many saw a reflection of George Orwell's *1984* in that and related surveillance. And the ACLU spokesperson asked, "What kind of society do we want to live in where everyone can be under surveillance, where as soon as you're named a suspect, police can monitor every move you make?" The Police responded by noting several cases in which cameras helped with investigation, with securing convictions, or in refuting allegations.

How did concern about drugs invade privacy?

Many people have felt strongly that drugs and drug use threatened society itself. In their urge to attack the drug problem, they advocated random drug testing. Such drug testing raised practical questions. Among these were the accuracy of the testing, the necessity of follow-up testing after the initial confirmation of drug use, care in labeling and controlling the samples as they were sent to be tested and results were reported, and the effects of false positive labeling of the nonuser as a user.

Beyond the practical issues were privacy issues as well as constitutional issues concerning unreasonable searches and seizures, self-incrimination, and due process. Especially important among privacy issues were those involved in random testing where there was no suspicion or reason to believe the individual had been using drugs, and those involved in discovering off-duty drug use where the individual had engaged in behavior which did not affect his work or others' performance. Those who took an individual rights-oriented approach strongly urged caution in invasions of privacy. Those who took a utilitarian-oriented approach, advocating society's concerns and placing safety issues paramount considered such invasions of privacy to be necessary.

What is neurolaw?

The use in the law of neuroscientific evidence from brain scans was termed neurolaw. Those scans were used to augment or make significant arguments. In defending those charged with crimes, the evidence was used to argue that offenders were not criminally responsible because their brains not their free will made them commit their acts. In legal briefs to the U.S. Supreme Court in the case of Roper v. Simmons, the evidence was used to argue that juveniles should be spared the death penalty because adolescent brains were not fully developed. In assessing moral decision making in response to two variants of a standard moral hypothetical, the evidence was used to show that different versions of the hypothetical caused different brain regions to become active. In one version, the brain regions associated with rational thought were active causing research subjects to make a utilitarian judgment; in another version, the brain regions associated with emotion were active causing research subjects to make an emotional judgment. One researcher concluded: "'This suggests that moral judgment is not a single thing; it's intuitive emotional responses and then cognitive responses that are duking it out.'"

What did skeptics conclude about the promise of neurolaw?

Skeptics and critics responded to the neuroscientists' claim that nothing caused behavior other than operation of the brain. One critic called that "brain over-claim syndrome." Critics focused on the many other factors that mediate between the brain and the behavior that results. One might, for example, hold racist thoughts, but behave in a non-racist way. Critics argued that issues like criminal responsibility required moral and legal decision making which might be influenced to some extent by brain scans but could not be controlled by them.

How did lie detection by polygraph invade privacy?

Drug testing remained but an aspect of the larger issue of lie detection. Drug testing would not be necessary if individuals would readily admit drug use or if polygraphs, lie detectors, were simple and effective means of detecting any drug use. Whereas drug tests were thought to be straightforward efforts to determine facts, lie detector tests were considered more difficult ways of ascertaining answers to important questions.

It was estimated that throughout the United States, about a half million employees and applicants for jobs were required each year to take polygraph examinations to obtain or to keep a job. More than a third of the Fortune 500 companies used the polygraph, because of concerns for security.

The polygraph was based on the theory that certain involuntary physiological responses were occasioned by lying. These were measured by the polygraph machine and included heartbeat, blood pressure, and respiration. Yet assessing these measures depended on the skill of the polygraph operator and those being tested could distort the record by distracting themselves, dissociating themselves from the questioning, rationalizing answers to questions, or by deliberately changing their responses through various means. Because of those problems and because of the considerable number of false positives, findings that a person was lying when the person was not, civil liberties lawyers and others argued against the use of polygraphs in most situations.

Arguments against the use of polygraphs included their ineffectiveness, in part because the testing situation itself may have caused such strong reaction to the invasion of privacy that it appeared that the person tested was lying when he was not; their masking of racial, sexual, and other forms of discrimination; and their contribution to the imbalance between the right of the prospective employer to screen potential employees for honesty and the right of the prospective employee to privacy. While the need to detect theft and to prevent hiring thieves was conceded by all, those who argued against polygraph examination of prospective employees suggested better background checks for job applicants or the use of undercover agents. Even those alternative methods risked the charge of invasion of privacy.

Those who considered lie detectors essential and argued to permit polygraph examinations often suggested using written consent forms, providing the applicant examinee with a verbatim statement of questions to be asked before they were asked, and eliminating questions about race, religion, political or labor views, sexual behavior or any event that occurred more than five or six or even seven years earlier.

How did lie detection by brain scan invade privacy?

While the polygraph relied on physiological measures, brain scans relied on fMRIs to examine directly the activation of areas of the brain. As Rosen pointed out, there were two lie-detection techniques that relied on that neuroimaging. One was termed "brain fingerprinting;" and the second compared the brain activity of liars and truth tellers. While researchers and companies marketing the tools made claims for the accuracy of the techniques, skeptics questioned their conclusions. Yet, Rosen reported, the Director of Neuroethics at the Stanford Center for Biomedical Ethics predicted that within half a decade these tests, unlike polygraphs, will be admissible in some legal contexts.

Efforts to expand the use of brain scans to potential jurors, and others drawn into the legal system will continue to raise ethical concerns about invasions of privacy. Perhaps, someday, there will be walk-through brain scans as there are now walk-through metal detectors. Those will really give increased cause for concern to advocates for privacy.

What might be said in conclusion about legal and moral decision making?

We end this book with a series of questions about moral decision making, for when it comes to *Thinking About Law and Ethics*, the questions we ask are at least as important as the answers we get. The questions continue and whether we attempt to answer in legal terms, based on the original intent of the Framers of the U.S. Constitution or on the evolving standards of decency; or in moral terms based on religion, on philosophical values, or on other ethical theories, the questions will continue; the advocates for the competing answers will continue; and each person and society will have to decide how to balance the competing claims. In that balance lie the contemporary problems in ethics and the law which we seek to address while we are thinking about legal and moral decision making.

Bibliography

Akron v. Akron Center for Reproductive Health 462 U.S. 416 (1983).

Ali, A. (2005). Unfree under Islam: Shariah endangers women's rights, from Iraq to Canada. *Wall Street Journal,* August 16.

Allen, S. (2007). McLean told to investigate former chief: State cites admission of sexual misconduct. *The Boston Globe*, October 11.

American Heritage Dictionary of the English Language (4th ed.) (2004). NY: Houghton Mifflin Co.

Atkins v. Virginia 536 U.S. 304 (2002).

Austen-Smith, D. and Fryer, R. (2005). An economic analysis of 'acting white.' *The Quarterly Journal of Economics*, May.

Ayotte v. Planned Parenthood of Northern New England 546 U.S. ___ (2006).

Barisic, S. (2006). Virginia teen who won court fight to forgo chemotherapy hopeful after cancer treatment in Mississippi. *Associated Press,* October 10.

Behnke, S. (2007). The work of the APA Ethics Office: Frequent calls we receive. *Monitor on Psychology,* September.

Bentham, J. (1996). *An Introduction to the Principles of Morals and Legislation.* NY: Oxford University Press.

Berger, R. (1999). *Death Penalties: The Supreme Court's obstacle course.* Lincoln, NE: iUniverse.

Berger, R. (1997). *Government by Judiciary: The transformation of the Fourteenth Amendment.* Indianapolis, IN: Liberty Fund.

Bernays, A. (1997). *Professor Romeo.* Lebanon, NH: University Press of New England.

Berns, W. (1991). *For Capital Punishment.* Lanham, MD: University Press of America.

Betts v. Brady 316 U.S. 455 (1942).

Black, C. (1981). *Capital Punishment: The inevitability of caprice and mistake.* NY: Norton.

Blackburn, S. (2001). *Being Good: A short introduction to ethics.* NY: Oxford University Press.

Bork, R. (1997). *The Tempting of America.* NY: Free Press.

Bork, R. (ed.). (2005). *A Country I Do Not Recognize: The legal assault on American values.* Stanford, CA: Hoover Institution Press.

Bowen, W., and Bok, D. (2000). *The Shape of the River: The long-term consequences of considering race in college and university admissions.* Princeton, NJ: Princeton University Press.

Bowers v. Hardwick 478 U.S. 186 (1986).

Bronner, E. (2007). *Battle for Justice: How the Bork nomination shook America.* NY: Union Square Press.

Brown v. Board of Education (I) 347 U.S. 483 (1954).

Brown v. Board of Education (II) 349 U.S. 294 (1955).

Burrough, B.and Helyar, J. (2003). *Barbarians at the Gate: The fall of RJR Nabisco.* NY: HarperCollins.

Connerly, W. (2002). *Creating Equal: My fight against race preferences.* NY: Encounter.

District Attorney for Suffolk District v. Watson 411 N.E.2nd 1274 (Mass.1980).

Damore, L. (1992). *The "Crime" of Dorothy Sheridan.* NY: Dell.

Dworkin, R. (1986). *A Matter of Principle.* Cambridge, MA: Harvard University Press.

Dworkin, R. (2005). *Taking Rights Seriously.* Cambridge, MA: Harvard University Press.

Dworkin, R. (2007). The Supreme Court phalanx. *The New York Review of Books*, September 27.

Dziech, B. and Weiner, L. (1990). *The Lecherous Professor: Sexual harassment on campus.* Champaign, IL: University of Illinois Press.

Falwell, J. (1980). *Listen, America!* NY: Bantam.

Faux, M. (1988). *Roe v. Wade.* NY: Signet.

Fersch, E. (1980). Ethical issues for psychologists in court settings. In Monahan, J. (ed.) *Who is the Client?* Washington, D.C.: American Psychological Association.

Fersch, E. (ed.). (2005.) *Thinking About the Insanity Defense: Answers to frequently asked questions with case examples.* Lincoln, NE: iUniverse.

Fersch, E. (ed.). (2006). *Thinking About the Sexually Dangerous: Answers to frequently asked questions with case examples.* Lincoln, NE: iUniverse.

Fersch, E. (ed.). (2006). *Thinking About Psychopaths and Psychopathy: Answers to frequently asked questions with case examples.* Lincoln, NE: iUniverse.

Fricke, A. (1981). *Reflections of a Rock Lobster.* Boston, MA: Alyson.

Furman v. Georgia 408 U.S. 238 (1972).

Fryer, R. (2005). Acting white: The social price paid by the best and brightest minority students. *Education Next*, Winter.

Gaylin, W, Kass, L, Pellegrino, E, and Siegler M. (1998). Doctors must not kill. *Journal of the American Medical Association,* April.

Gideon v. Wainwright 372 U.S. 335 (1963).

Gill, G. (1999). *Mary Baker Eddy.* Cambridge, MA: Da Capo.

Golden, D. (2007). *The Price of Admission: How America's ruling class buys its way into elite colleges—and who gets left outside the gates.* NY: Three Rivers Press.

Gonzales v. Carhart 550 U.S. ___ (2007).

Gonzales v. Oregon 546 U.S. ___ (2006).

Gonzales v. Planned Parenthood 550 U.S. ___ (2007).

Goodridge v. Department of Public Health 798 N.E.2d 941 (Mass. 2003).

Gratz v. Bollinger 539 U.S. 244 (2003).

Gregg v. Georgia 428 U.S. 153 (1976).

Grutter v. Bollinger 529 U.S. 306 (2003).

Haidt, J. (2006). *The Happiness Hypothesis*. NY: Basic Books.

Hanlon, S. (2005). Lack of public defenders overwhelming courts. *The Boston Globe*, July 19.

Harr, J. (1995). *A Civil Action*. NY: Vintage.

Harvard Law Review (1990). *Sexual Orientation and the Law*. Cambridge, MA: Harvard University Press.

Iran: Two more executions for homosexual conduct. (2005). *Human Rights News*, November 22.

Irons, P. (1990). *The Courage of Their Convictions: Sixteen Americans who fought their way to the Supreme Court*. NY: Penguin.

Kant, I. (1998). *Groundwork of the Metaphysics of Morals*. NY: Cambridge University Press.

Kennedy, R. (2003). *Nigger: The strange career of a troublesome word*. NY: Vintage.

Kennedy, R. (2007) *Sellout: The politics of racial betrayal*. NY: Pantheon.

Kevorkian, J. (1993). *Prescription Medicide: The goodness of planned death*. Amherst, NY: Prometheus.

Kluger, R. (2004). *Simple Justice: The history of Brown v Board of Education and black America's struggle for equality.* NY: Vintage.

Krasner, J. (2006). Christian Science provision sought in healthcare law. *The Boston Globe,* August 28.

Kugel, J. (2007). *How to Read the Bible: A guide to scripture, then and now.* NY: Free Press.

Lawrence and Garner v. Texas 539 U.S. 558 (2003).

Lewis, A. (1964). *Gideon's Trumpet.* NY: Vintage.

Lewis, A. (2004). The Court v. Bush. *The New York Times,* June 29.

Lewis, A. (2005). Guantanamo's long shadow. *The New York Times,* June 21.

Lewis, H. (2000). *A Question of Values: Six ways we make the personal choices that shape our lives.* Mount Jackson, VA: Axios Press.

Lilla, M. (2007). The politics of God. *The New York Times Magazine,* August 19.

Lilla, M. (2007). *The Stillborn God: Religion, politics, and the modern world.* NY: Knopf.

Luker, K. (1985). *Abortion and the Politics of Motherhood.* Berkeley, CA: University of California Press.

Massey, D., Mooney, M., Charles, C., and Torres, K. (2007). Black immigrants and black natives attending selective colleges and universities in the United States. *American Journal of Education, February (113, 2), 243-271.*

McCorvey, N. (1995*). I Am Roe: My life, Roe v. Wade, and freedom of choice.* NY: Perennial.

McWhorter, J. (2001). *Losing the Race: Self-sabotage in black America.* NY: Harper.

Meredith v. Jefferson County Board of Education 551 U.S. ___ (2007).

Mill, J. (2005). *On Liberty.* Indianapolis, IN: Hackett Publishing.

Mill, J. (2002). *Utilitarianism.* Indianapolis, IN: Hackett Publishing.

Mokhiber, R. (1988). *Corporate Crimes and Violence: Big business power and the abuse of public trust.* NY: Random House.

Mukasey, M. (2004). Before attacking the Patriot Act, try reading it. *Wall Street Journal,* May 10.

Nesteruk, J. (2005). The limits of law as a moral arbiter. *The Chronicle Review,* September 16.

Oregon (2005). Statutes Chapter 127—Powers of Attorney; Advance Directives for Health Care; Declarations for Mental Health Treatment; Death with Dignity.

Parents Involved in Community Schools v. Seattle School District No. 1 551 U.S. ___ (2007).

Planned Parenthood v. Casey. 505 U.S. 833 (1992).

Privacy impact assessment for the Automated Targeting System. (2006). *U.S. Department of Homeland Security,* November.

Putnam, R. (2007). E Pluribus Unum: Diversity and community in the twenty-first century: The 2006 Johan Skytte prize lecture. *Scandinavian Political Studies,* June.

Rawls, J. (2005). *A Theory of Justice.* Cambridge, MA: Harvard University Press.

Rawls, J. (2005). *Political Liberalism.* NY: Columbia University Press.

Rawls, J. and Kelly, E. (2001). *Justice as Fairness: A restatement.* Cambridge, MA: Harvard University Press.

Reed, M. (2007). Virginia teen who won court fight needs more cancer treatment. *Associated Press,* January 6.

Regents of the University of California v. Bakke 438 U.S. 265 (1978).

Roe v. Wade 410 U.S. 113 (1973).

Rollin, B. (1998). *Last Wish.* NY: Public Affairs.

Roper v. Simmons 543 U.S. 551 (2005).

Rose, R. (author), Lumet, S. (director). (1957). *12 Angry Men.*

Rosen, J. (2007). Neurolaw: The brain on the stand. *The New York Times Magazine*, March 11.

Saltzman, J. (2007). Judge chastised for vacating assault conviction: 'Deviation from laws of Commonwealth.' *The Boston Globe*, October 11.

Sander, R. (2004). "A systemic analysis of affirmative action in American law schools." *Stanford Law Review,* November.

Sander, R. (2005). A reply to critics. *Stanford Law Review* (57, 6), 1963-2016, May.

Saxe, R. (2005). Do the right thing: Cognitive science's search for a common morality. *Boston Review,* September-October.

Schur, E. and Bedau, H. (1975). *Victimless Crimes.* NY: Prentice Hall.

Scruton, R. (2006). 'Islamofascism:' Beware of a religion without irony. *The Wall Street Journal,* August 20.

Schenck v. United States 249 U.S. 47 (1919).

Schmidt, P. (2007). *Color and Money: How rich white kids are winning the war over college affirmative action.* NY: Palgrave Macmillan.

Shubow, L. (1986). Inquest: Death of Robin Twitchell. West Roxbury, Massachusetts District Court.

Silberger, J. (1980). *Mary Baker Eddy: An interpretive biography of the founder of Christian Science.* Boston, MA: Little, Brown.

Singer, P. (1999). *Practical Ethics.* NY: Cambridge University Press.

Starr, P. (2007). *Freedom's Power: The true force of liberalism.* NY: Perseus.

Steele, S. (1991). *The Content of Our Character: A new vision of race in America.* NY: Harper.

Taylor, S. and Johnson, K. (2007). *Until Proven Innocent: Political correctness and the shameful injustices of the Duke lacrosse rape case.* NY: Thomas Dunne/St. Martin's.

"The Pope must die," says Muslim. (2006). *This Is London,* September 18.

Thernstrom, A. (2007). The massacre of innocence. *Wall Street Journal,* September 6.

Thernstrom, S. (2000). One-drop still. A racialist Census. *The National Review,* April 17.

Toobin, J. (2007). *The Nine: Inside the secret world of the Supreme Court.* NY: Doubleday.

Tribe, L. (1992). *Abortion: The clash of absolutes.* NY: Norton.

Turow, S. (2004). *Ultimate Punishment: A lawyer's reflections on dealing with the death penalty.* NY: Picador.

Uttecht v. Brown 551 U.S. ___ (2007).

Walker, H. (2007). Why are the media so angry at Clarence Thomas? *The Boston Globe,* October 11.

Warren, S. and Brandeis, L. (1890). The right to privacy. *Harvard Law Review,* December.

Webster v. Reproductive Health Services. 492 U.S. 490 (1989).

Weisberg, R. (1995). Some ways to think about law reviews. *Stanford Law Review,* Summer.

Wiechman, D., Kendall, J., and Azarian, M. (2005). Shariah Islamic law. *Office of International Criminal Justice at the University of Illinois,* April 7.

Wilkinson, J. (1979). *From Brown to Bakke: The Supreme Court and school integration, 1954-1978.* NY: Oxford University Press.

Wills, G. (2007). *Head and Heart: American Christianities.* NY: Penguin.

Wilson, J. (2007). Bowling with others. *Commentary,* October.

Wright, J. (1990). *On a Clear Day You Can See General Motors.* NY: Avon.

978-0-595-47673-2
0-595-47673-2

www.ingramcontent.com/pod-product-compliance
Lightning Source LLC
Chambersburg PA
CBHW030941180526
45163CB00002B/664